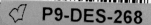

special
needs
special
ministry

for children's ministry

contributing authors

jim **Pierson**

louise **Tucker Jones**

pat **Verbal**

foreword by
Joni Eareckson Tada

Group
Loveland, Colorado

Group's R.E.A.L. Guarantee® to you:

This Group resource incorporates our R.E.A.L. approach to ministry—one that encourages long-term retention and life transformation. It's ministry that's:

Relational
Because learner-to-learner interaction enhances learning and builds Christian friendships.

Experiential
Because what learners experience through discussion and action sticks with them up to 9 times longer than what they simply hear or read.

Applicable
Because the aim of Christian education is to equip learners to be both hearers and doers of God's Word.

Learner-based
Because learners understand and retain more when the learning process takes into consideration how they learn best.

Special Needs—Special Ministry
Copyright © 2004

Visit our Web site: **www.grouppublishing.com**

Credits
Editor: Mikal Keefer
Chief Creative Officer: Joani Schultz
Copy Editor: Janis Sampson
Art Director: Randy Kady
Cover Art Director and Designer: Bambi Eitel
Print Production Artist: Lynn Gardner
Cover Photographer: Joshua Fletcher
Production Manager: Peggy Naylor

Unless otherwise noted, Scripture taken from the HOLY BIBLE, NEW INTERNATIONAL VERSION®. Copyright © 1973, 1978, 1984 by International Bible Society. Used by permission of Zondervan Publishing House. All rights reserved.

Library of Congress Cataloging-in-Publication Data
Special needs, special ministry.-- 1ˢᵗ American pbk. ed.
     p. cm.
Includes bibliographical references.
ISBN 0-7644-2547-1 (pbk. : alk. paper)
1. Parents of children with disabilities—Religious life. 2. Church work with families.
  I. Group Publishing.
BV4596.P35S68 2003
259'.4--dc22
    2003014772

10 9 8 7 6 5 4 3 2 1   13 12 11 10 09 08 07 06 05 04
Printed in the United States of America.

Table of Contents

108893

special needs—special ministry
for children's ministry

Before You Begin—A Word From Joni Eareckson Tada

Dear Friend,

When a diving accident in 1967 robbed me of the use of my hands and legs, I found myself in a hospital ward wondering if I would ever smile and be hopeful again. I had become just statistical data—a member of the population affected by disabilities. And I was dangerously close to becoming a number on the list of the depressed.

The darkness lifted when friends from my church rallied around my family, offering help, hope, and positive meaning for my life. It was the church that kept us connected to reality, opening doors of possibility and paving the way for me to re-enter the mainstream of life. The church made all the difference.

Unfortunately, my story is not unique. This is why, more than thirty-five years later, I'm pleased to labor alongside a worldwide staff of skilled and gifted individuals at Joni and Friends who are committed to accelerating Christian outreach into the disability community around the globe. We're energized by Jesus' statement in Luke 14:13-14a, 23b: "But when you give a banquet, invite the poor, the crippled, the lame, the blind, and you will be blessed. Make them come in, so that my house will be full."

Yes, we're convinced that people with disabilities will be blessed, but the key is that *you* will be blessed. When local churches such as yours reach beyond the comfort zones and embrace families with special needs children, the entire fellowship is blessed in dramatic ways. Your church will realize that we're richer when we recognize our poverty, we're stronger when we see our weaknesses, and we become recipients of God's grace when we understand our desperate need of him.

The book you hold in your hands, *Special Needs—Special Ministry*, is a wonderful key to unlocking the door to those blessings. As you turn each page, you'll discover practical steps on how to invite people with

disabilities and their families into the fold of Christ's fellowship. You'll also read stories that will inspire and encourage you as you embark into the exciting world of disability ministry outreach.

So thank you for stepping out in this new pathway to blessing. May your heart beat in rhythm with the Savior's as you enjoy reading *Special Needs—Special Ministry,* and may God grant success as you put into practice all that you glean. After all, a ministry to special needs children and their families involves not only a change for the family, it means a change in your church and your community. Most of all, it's about a change in *you*—for as you shine God's light and shake his salt, as you open up new doors of access in your church, as you reach out, one thing is sure: You *will* be blessed.

Joni Eareckson Tada is founder and president of Joni and Friends, an organization accelerating Christian ministry in the disability community. Joni is a best-selling author, artist, and speaker. Her role as a disability advocate led to a presidential appointment to the National Council on Disability for three and one-half years, during which time the Americans with Disabilities Act became law.

1. Why Your Church Needs a Special Needs Ministry

by Pat Verbal

These days it seems people expect their church to provide a staggering array of specialized ministries.

People want ministries for women. For men. For singles. For young marrieds. For people who've been divorced. For families. For children. For the elderly. Sometimes pastors and other church staff wonder if there's any group of three or more people that *hasn't* convinced a local church to develop a program to meet their needs.

Well, yes, there *is* such a group.

I belong to it.

Let me share my story...

The Longest Flight

As a Christian education consultant and speaker, I spend a lot of time on airplanes. But no flight has felt longer than the one I took a few years ago from San Francisco to Texas.

I'd visited a mission-style bungalow in a crowded San Francisco suburb, then rushed to the airport—in tears.

As I sat on the airplane, I silently praised God for answering my prayer— I'd been able to visit our precious Jessica, age twelve, who has Down

syndrome. Yet, I was flying home alone. Jessica had to remain in the group home where she'd been placed for reasons beyond our control.

This sweet child who'd brought so much fun into our home was alone, growing up without her family. Growing up in a world she'd never understand.

Fighting back the tears I prayed, *Lord, why can't I bring her home with me?*

When Jessica was two years old, she'd become part of my extended family. She instantly stole our hearts and spent many happy days in our home.

Fighting back the tears I prayed, *Lord, why can't I bring her home with me?*

Jessica had always been small for her age, behind the norm in every area of her development. Still, she could get a roomful of adults on their feet singing "Ring Around the Rosie," and the song never ended until everyone fell down. And bedtime was always interesting because Jessica never quite understood that once you were tucked in you were supposed to *stay* in bed. She got giddy when she was tired. Many nights she laughed herself to sleep.

I missed those bedtimes. I ached for them.

Lord, why can't I bring her home with me?

At first Jessica's mother had been determined to raise Jessica in a loving, Christian home. She tried hard—very hard—but the task was too over-whelming. She struggled with exhaustion, mood swings, and depression. Eventually she gave up on her marriage, her faith, and her daughter. That's when she placed Jessica in the group home.

As I flew back to Texas that fall afternoon, I tried to tell myself that Jessica was fine. The group home was clean and orderly. The house-mother liked Jessica and wanted her to be happy. Jessica had proudly sung her ABCs for me, then showed me Opra, a rag doll I'd given her, perched on Jessica's bedroom pillow. Opra had been a faithful friend to Jessica, more faithful than some of the adults in her life.

Lord, why can't I bring her home with me?

So there I was, wounded, flying home to a house that no longer held my precious little one.

In San Francisco Jessica needed the church to wrap its arms around her, welcome her, and hold her close. And headed to Texas was a weeping woman—me—who needed the same thing.

Would Jessica be welcomed and understood in your church?

Would Jessica's birth mother?

Would I?

The Need for Special Needs Ministries

According to the National Organization on Disability, there are fifty-four million people in the United States with disabilities. That means one in five Americans has a disability of some sort. One in five! And a significant number of those people with disabilities are children like Jessica.

I'd love to tell you the church at large is doing a wonderful job responding to these children, but I can't. Too many parents have disappointing stories to share…

- Belinda called several churches in town when her daughter, Ellen, turned two years old. Cognitive and seizure disorders had kept Ellen at home since birth, and Belinda felt it was important for Ellen to have social contact with other children.

  Belinda was shocked to discover that two churches wouldn't allow Ellen to be in Sunday school at all. A third church accepted Ellen but put her in the baby nursery. When Belinda picked Ellen up, she discovered that the volunteer had left her daughter sitting in a swing the entire time.

- Kevin's experience with his son, Sammy, didn't turn out even that well.

  Sammy, an active seven-year-old, was mildly autistic. About half the time Sammy was in Sunday school, Kevin and his wife were called out of church to pick Sammy up. The teachers simply couldn't handle Sammy's behavior.

  Most Sundays Kevin and his wife felt like staying home and watching the service on television.

- And imagine Pam's response when she was told her three-year-old son, Jacob, was "a little spoiled." Jacob had many sensory issues, including a strong gag reflex. This caused him to vomit frequently, especially when crying or coughing. The teacher suggested that Jacob may have vomited on purpose, just to get the class's attention.

Children with disabilities too often find that the church doesn't truly welcome or truly value them. There simply isn't a place for these children when kids scamper off to Sunday school classes on Sunday morning.

And the children aren't the only ones who suffer.

According to Dr. Jim Pierson, president of the Christian Church Foundation for the Handicapped, families that have children with disabilities can quickly find themselves in crisis.

special needs—special ministry
for children's ministry

There's a high rate of divorce and desertion in these families. Extra costs associated with caring for children with disabilities can severely impact family finances and create tremendous stress. The siblings of children with special needs often find it difficult to adjust.

The challenges of raising children with special needs are overwhelming, and many families face those challenges without the church's intentional, active involvement.

The help these families and children need begins with Sunday school classes that welcome the children. That alone would be a tremendous blessing. This book will help you accomplish that task by providing practical steps you can follow and introducing you to Christian education leaders like you who have made the journey.

And along the way you'll also be challenged to consider what you might do *beyond* Sunday morning. What can you do to provide a listening, understanding ear to a mother whose life revolves around the treatment and care of a child with special needs? How can you help the sister of that child deal with her parents' preoccupation? How can you surround that family with the love of Christ?

Maybe you're thinking that other churches in your community are already caring for special needs children and their families, and there's no need for you to get involved.

Sadly, you'd be wrong.

Are Churches Serving Special Needs Children and Their Families?

No one knows how many churches are actively, intentionally reaching out to special needs children and their families. But I think my own neighborhood is a good indication.

I live in the Dallas metropolitan area, and we have no shortage of churches. In the Greater Dallas Southwestern Bell Yellow Pages, there are fifteen pages of churches listed. I figure that comes to approximately 2,600 churches.

The ads for churches list many ministries—worship services, choirs, hand-bell choirs, Bible studies, retreats, children's programs, youth ministries, sports and recreation ministries, recovery ministries, even a cappuccino ministry.

But not one ad highlights a special needs ministry.

I know for a fact that several area churches do have programs, but newcomers to the Dallas area will apparently have to find those churches by word of mouth.

In contrast, the Yellow Pages list eleven schools for special needs children, nineteen service organizations, and page after page of medical centers specializing in a wide variety of disabilities.

Open up your town's Yellow Pages. What do see there? Is there any indication that the church is a resource to families with special needs children? When you think of churches in your area and your own church, how do you rank the body of Christ as a source of hope and caring for these families?

I believe there's room for improvement. Lots of room. This book will describe how your church can launch—or grow—a special needs ministry to children and their families.

But before we dive into the practical how to's, let's dispel several myths...

"Our church doesn't need a special needs ministry because there aren't any special needs children in our area."

Don't think so? Pick up the phone, and call three or four elementary schools in your area. Ask if there are children with disabilities who attend. Then call the facilities you find in your Yellow Pages that exist specifically to work with special needs children.

Here's the truth: The children and their families are out there. They just may not have come to your church because you have little to offer. And if you're offering a special needs ministry, they may not have heard about you yet because you're not letting people know about your ministry.

"To do a special needs ministry, we need to be a big church."

The size of your church isn't important. It's the size of your *heart* that counts. If you believe that the Great Commission applies to everyone—including children in wheelchairs—then what are you waiting for? How can you *not* design your programming and outreach to include families who need the light and fellowship of your congregation?

"Special needs kids would never fit into our programming."

Sure they will! If your goal is to include children into existing classes and programs, there's probably a way to do so by simply adapting your programs, not changing them radically.

special needs—special ministry
for children's ministry

One church I know has a children's music program. The children in that church who have Down syndrome love to sing—and the choir director has arranged music that allows them to participate in making a joyful noise to the Lord.

Another church has a ministry that teaches children how to swim in a community pool. That's not an ideal fit for every child with a disability, but it works for many of the children. Whatever your programming, there's probably a way to accommodate children who have special needs. See Chapter 2 for some recommendations about how to make the adjustments.

"We'll have to spend a fortune fixing our building."

Not so. If your building was designed and built after 1990 in the United States, it was probably designed with the ADA in mind. That means doorways are wide enough to accommodate wheelchairs and many barriers that interfered with the mobility of people with disabilities have been removed.

But even if you meet in an older facility, it's doubtful you'll have to do much to accommodate children with disabilities and their families. You're not legally required to install elevators or retrofit bathrooms; religious organizations are exempt from the ADA's title III requirements for public accommodations—*so long as you use the building only for worship.*

If any other event takes place in the building—such as a community group meeting, day care, or hosting concerts or luncheons—the ADA standards apply. If you have any questions about your facility, call the ADA Information Line at 800-514-0301 and check.

That means it's possible your church building won't be held to the same standards a government building or bank has to meet. But—and here's a question for you to ponder—why would you want to do any less?

The point of the ADA was to remove barriers that kept people from participating fully in community life. As Christians, we're all about involving people in our community of faith. Some of that happens inside the buildings where we meet. Let's not keep people out if building a wheelchair ramp will allow them in.

"Special needs kids can get their needs met elsewhere. That's what group homes are for."

I thank God for caring, well-run group homes. And for the professionals who meet children's other physical needs—they're tremendous individuals.

But in many instances a group home isn't the church. Teaching children about God isn't part of the daily routine or even part of the home's mission statement.

Expecting most group homes to encourage children to know, love, and follow Jesus would be like expecting the hospital where you go for minor surgery to also care as deeply about your spiritual health. The doctors don't even *think* about that; they're focused on removing your appendix or fixing your knee.

The church can't delegate its responsibility for nurturing the faith of children to outside agencies. Rather, we need to work with parents to assume their God-given role as primary faith shapers and cooperate with the work God is doing in the hearts of children.

"We don't have anyone here who can handle special needs kids."

It's true that working with children who are "different" requires some training. But working with special needs children doesn't require a degree in special education. Or a teaching certificate. In this book you'll read about churches that launched effective ministries with little or no experience beyond a desire to serve children and a heart for God. There's ample opportunity for training from community agencies, parents of special needs kids, and mentoring from professionals.

Don't let the lack of a training program slow you down. Chapter 7 suggests ways you can quickly get your staff and volunteers up to speed. If you're a typical church, there's nothing stopping you from reaching out to special needs kids and their families through a special needs ministry.

Nothing but a decision to do so.

What Exactly Is a "Special Needs Ministry"?

A special needs ministry is simply a ministry aimed at meeting the spiritual needs of children who have disabilities.

The mission statement of the special needs ministry at the Golden Hills Community Church in Brentwood, California, sums it up well: "To make disciples within the disabled community by demonstrating Christ's love and equipping the congregation to minister to their special needs so that all might fellowship, worship, and serve."

Special needs are disabilities that prevent children from progressing mentally, physically, or emotionally at the customary pace. The disabilities themselves are extremely diverse, but many share common symptoms. If you create a special needs ministry, you can count on at least some of your students demonstrating…

- hyperactivity with short attention spans
- distractibility and impulsiveness
- poor visual/motor skills and poor large muscle and fine motor coordination
- rapid and excessive changes of mood and reasoning
- faulty perception with repetition of a thought or action
- problems with social interaction and inconsistent and unpredictable behavior

Will these be the "easiest" children you have involved in your church program? Probably not…but they may well be the most willing to learn. The most willing to serve. The most willing to share God's love with family and friends.

And they may well make a significant difference in your church and the world as they live out their faith.

Mark Thompson is a gifted musical ventriloquist who was an ADD (attention-deficit disorder) child. "I'm often asked how I carry on a lively conversation with a puppet on each hand," says Mark. "I tell people that's just the way my mind works. I function best when I'm focused and going full speed ahead."

> As a child Mark was hyperactive, loud, and describes himself as "often annoying."

As a child Mark was hyperactive, loud, and describes himself as "often annoying." He wanted to learn, but found it hard to control himself and to stop talking. In spite of his behavior, his teachers at church managed to make him feel loved and accepted.

"My father also had problems in school because he couldn't read well," says Mark. "People called him a dummy. So instead of finishing high school, he worked in a garden," The only book that Mark ever saw his father pick up was the Bible.

Mark is thankful for mentors who gave him love and guidance. He prays for children with ADD to know God. "I entertain thousands of people each year and train church teachers to plug these kids in with responsibility, structure, and ownership. They can shine for Jesus."

A special needs ministry would welcome Mark, valuing him. And it would provide a shoulder on which his weary parents could lean for support.

That's ultimately a decision you'll need to make for yourself, but consider this summary of a document the National Council of Churches General Assembly accepted in 1998. Does it ring true with your understanding of biblical truth?

1. All people are created in the image of God (Genesis 1:26). This image is not a measurable set of characteristics. God's image is reflected uniquely in each person.

2. All people are called by God (Ephesians 2:10). Disabilities in no way preclude someone from being valued by God.

3. All people have special gifts (1 Corinthians 12:4). The gifts God has given each person are needed by all other people, and no one is unnecessary.

4. All people are invited to participate in God's ministry (1 Corinthians 12:7). God continually empowers each member of the body of Christ to serve and benefit the church and the broader community.

5. And may I add a few verses for your consideration? In Matthew 19:14 we see Jesus call children to himself. And

(continued)

What Will a Special Needs Ministry Do for Your Church?

For starters, you'll be fulfilling the Great Commission.

Nowhere in Jesus' command that the gospel be shared with the world does he add a qualifier that only the able-bodied need be contacted. If anything, Jesus showed a special compassion for the ill, the lame, those who might be candidates for a special needs ministry.

While visiting a church in Alabama, I was escorted by the pastor to a front-row seat. That's when I noticed the young people filling the pew next to me. Many of them had Down syndrome. Others were in wheelchairs. I returned their smiles and waves as the organist began to play.

The young people were obviously delighted with their special spot. During the worship music, a girl picked up her papers and moved to a new seat. A boy held his songbook upside down and sang off key, but with gusto. Another rushed down the aisle, talked to a gentleman, and scurried back to his place. During greeting time, I was bombarded by handshakes and hugs. I couldn't understand their words, but their enthusiasm brought tears to my eyes.

I couldn't help but notice how loving the pastors were to their "front-row crowd." Many in the congregation also took extra care to greet them and engage in conversation.

This was so different from what I'm used to seeing in churches that I asked the pastor about it. "If Jesus were alive today," he said, "we believe he would be leading a special needs ministry. He had such a heart for those who seemed to get left out."

Who wouldn't want their church to be a place like that? Where nobody gets left out?

You'll reflect God's love in your community.

A common criticism of the church is that it simply isn't relevant. It preaches but has no pulse, no connection to real life. That's certainly not the case when you're meeting real, felt needs like those of children with special needs and their families.

(continued from page 16) there's nothing he said or did here or elsewhere in his ministry that would suggest children couldn't be on crutches or in wheelchairs, developmentally disabled, or victims of abuse. He welcomed them all. Can we do less?

Nella Uitvlugt, Director of Friendship Ministries in Michigan, helps churches start well-rounded special needs ministries. Part of what she does is convince churches to see their ministries as resources for families as a whole. Noting that adults who had a sibling with a disability carry baggage from that situation into adulthood, she says, "Let's deal with these family issues while children are young. Some siblings may have to do more baby-sitting than other kids. They may not be able to participate in outside activities because there just isn't time, energy, and money to go around."

Your special needs ministry is more than simply a ministry to children—though that would be reason enough for your church to support a ministry. You'll also support parents, siblings, and families as a whole.

You'll invite some astonishing people into your midst.

During praise and worship one Sunday, out of the corner of my eye I saw Helen heading straight toward me. Clutching a piece of typing paper tightly in her fist, she wrapped her arms around my neck, gave me a quick hug, pushed the paper into my hand, and bounced back to her seat.

Looking down I saw green, red, blue, and yellow hearts drawn with a shaky hand. The large, out-of-proportion print read, "To Pat from Helen for Valentines. I love you."

Helen is a petite young woman who blesses our church. Her speech is difficult to understand, but she clearly embodies the childlike faith Jesus described in Luke 18:16b-17: "For the Kingdom of God belongs to men [and women] who have hearts as trusting as these little children's. And anyone who doesn't have their kind of faith will never get within the Kingdom's gates" (The Living Bible).

You'll grow a generation of children who are tolerant and accepting of people with special needs.

As your typical children interact with peers who have special needs, you'll see walls come down...fear subside...curiosity be replaced by compassion. You'll disciple the children who *don't* have special needs to see that God doesn't make mistakes, that the kingdom of God includes people who are different than them, but who are still brothers and sisters in the Lord.

You'll assimilate families into your church.

If you start a special needs ministry, it's highly unlikely you'll suddenly double the size of your congregation. Special needs ministries don't attract large groups of people—but they will attract families that will bless you for your focus and ministry.

Families with special needs children have lessons to teach us. Disabilities have the power to draw families toward God's grace. Churches that reach out to these families and their children are promised a blessing in return. "But when you give a banquet, invite the poor, the crippled, the lame, the blind, and you will be blessed" (Luke 14:13-14a).

Seek Understanding First

In many ways, a special needs ministry is much like any effective ministry: It must include an understanding of the people we wish to serve. Children with special needs, of course, but also their families.

Mary Ann McPherson can help us better appreciate what life is like when you live in a world of special needs around the clock. She's a Christian educator and also the mother of a young lady with Down syndrome.

Mary Ann will describe the life she and her family lead, then you'll dive into the nuts and bolts of what it takes to establish or expand a church-based special needs ministry.

But first, take a few moments to reflect on your ministry. Throughout this book you'll find "Just For You" sections. Don't skip past these brief passages. Think of them as quick opportunities to pause, be refreshed, and to let God speak to you about the unfolding ministry you're doing together.

Just for You

We often see images of Jesus hanging on the cross. He's usually pictured bloodied and battered, grimacing in pain. Yet he looks down with a compassion that shines straight from his breaking heart.

Think about that scene from a different perspective for a moment. Think about who's standing *beneath* the cross, scattered across the hillside, looking up.

A mother watching her son die, one inch at a time, yet unable to help him.

A shattered man who has betrayed his closest friend.

A Roman soldier just now beginning to sense that an innocent man hangs silhouetted against the darkening sky, nailed to fierce, blood-stained wood.

Perhaps a man who once was hopelessly crippled, but who now could walk the crooked path up to the Place of the Skull.

There was room for all these people at the foot of the cross. There's room there for everyone. It doesn't matter if a person arrives on foot or in a wheelchair. Whether the person stands sightless, unable to hear, or unable to speak.

There's room for us all.

Thanks for reaching across the obstacles that special needs can create to share the message: There's room for you.

Dear God,

You love us all. Thank you for the chance to reach out with the good news to children with special needs and their families: There's room for us all at the foot of the cross. And there's room for us all in our church.

In Jesus' name, amen.

2. What Do Families With Special Needs Children Need?

by Mary Ann McPherson

Sarah is nine years old, the youngest of our three daughters. She has silky blonde hair. Big blue eyes. A charming, ear-to-ear smile.

And Sarah has Down syndrome.

From the moment a neonatal specialist told us there might be a genetic problem with Sarah, I sensed that every person in my life—family, friends, neighbors, and even acquaintances—were being drawn together in a circle around our family.

When our first two daughters were born, it was a circle of celebration.

This time it was a circle of concern.

And in a way we'd never experienced before, my husband and I became vulnerable and needy.

We Needed to Grieve

When a family discovers their child has a disability, it's often a time of crisis. There's no timetable for how long it takes to work through the news, but many family members go through the predictable stages of grief: denial, bargaining, anger, depression, and eventual acceptance.

Parents and other close family members mourn the child they imagined would be born. A young mother once told me, "The moment the doctors said, 'It's a girl,' my thoughts raced with visions of ballet lessons, proms, academic scholarships, and a wedding dress. Then I heard the words *Down syndrome,* and all those dreams were shattered."

For many parents, like this mom, there's a time when their child's disability overshadows the very essence of the person God created in their child.

For some parents, grief becomes part of their life for years. Birthdays become a reminder of a child's lagging development. Meeting a nondisabled child who's the same age sets off unwelcome comparisons. Watching a younger child grow and develop beyond an older sibling is a painful reminder.

The first few months following a diagnosis of "disability" can be an emotionally fragile time for parents. These parents need helpful friends who'll be examples of Proverbs 18:24b: "There is a friend who sticks closer than a brother."

My husband, Dave, and I had some of those friends in our lives. They cooked for us, hugged us, and told us that they loved us. They acted as a buffer by passing on information. They gave us permission to cry and watched our other daughters when Sarah had medical appointments.

They listened and treated Sarah like any other newborn.

And most importantly, they prayed for us daily as we grieved.

We Needed to Survive the Emotional Roller Coaster

Here's what you can assume is true for any parent whose young child has a disability: That parent is emotionally drained.

The parents of an infant facing open-heart surgery shared, "We bounced from feeling peaceful and accepting of the place God had us into a total panic about the future, feeling that God had abandoned us. There were days we couldn't see past the day of surgery, and then there were days we worried about what life would be like for all of us in forty years."

Parents' emotions are filtered through the way they perceive a specific disability. That means what they know—or think they know—can have a huge impact on how they feel.

Other factors that impact a parent's response include their personal experiences with disabled persons. Have those experiences been positive or negative? Also, how well-grounded is the parent spiritually? What sort of support is the parent receiving from friends and family? Life becomes

Welcome to Holland
by Emily Perl Kingsley

I am often asked to describe the experience of raising a child with a disability—to try to help people who have not shared that unique experience to understand it, to imagine how it would feel. It's like this...

When you're going to have a baby, it's like planning a fabulous vacation trip—to Italy. You buy a bunch of guidebooks and make your wonderful plans. The Coliseum. The Michelangelo David. The gondolas in Venice. You may learn some handy phrases in Italian. It's all very exciting.

After months of eager anticipation, the day finally arrives. You pack your bags and off you go. Several hours later, the plane lands. The stewardess comes in and says, "Welcome to Holland."

"Holland?" you say. "What do you mean Holland? I signed up for Italy! I'm supposed to be in Italy. All my life I've dreamed of going to Italy."

But there's been a change in the flight plan. They've landed in Holland and there you must stay.

The important thing is that they haven't taken you to a horrible, disgusting, filthy place full

(continued)

---

emotionally complicated when parents feel it's necessary to comfort others or defend their beliefs about disabilities.

It was difficult for me to face our neighbors and church family the first few months after Sarah was born. I felt so unsteady at any given moment.

I also quickly discovered that some people were so uncomfortable with Sarah that they avoided us. Others poured out their sympathy. Still others were encouraging.

I know there are parents of special needs children who take a deep breath when they hear a diagnosis, then they move on without hesitation. But that wasn't me. I needed to grieve deeply, and my husband and dearest friends gave me the time and support to do so. Through my tears and prayers, I found that God was closer than he had ever been in my life. I knew for certain I was not alone and that God would give me wisdom and strength whenever I called on him.

Parents whose child has been diagnosed with a disability sometimes go through long periods of denial. They believe their child is only mildly affected and with a little therapy will be fine.

But then if the child doesn't develop as they had hoped, these parents sink into deep grief. They come to understand their hopes won't be rewarded, that their assumptions were incorrect.

That what they asked God to do isn't going to happen.

I Wrote This Entry in My Journal When Sarah Was Twelve Days Old:

Diane, our neighbor who's also a member of our church, came over late this afternoon with a baby gift. She oohed and aahed over Sarah and asked enthusiastically to hold her. I nervously explained the details of Sarah's birth and at the end I blurted out, "She has Down syndrome."

"I've heard that," replied Diane. This news was no big deal for her. She treated my baby as she would any other baby. I felt so encouraged. She gave me a copy of "Welcome to Holland."

Then came the tears. I cried because I want so desperately to see the joys that Sarah will bring. And I cried because I still don't want to be here.

Grief takes whatever time it takes. Are you allowing families whose children are disabled to take the time they need to grieve?

We Needed to Face the Unknown—and Our Fear

Parents of a child with a disability are quickly ushered into a foreign world.

It's the world of hospitals and medical specialists. A world that may include cardiologists, orthopedic specialists, genetic specialists, neurologists, physical therapists, occupational therapists, and early intervention specialists. A world crowded with medical appointments and frustrated with insurance forms no one can understand, no one can fill out perfectly.

And a world in which there's no way parents can know how their child's disability will impact the future—their child's future and their family's future.

We all feel concern about how our children will fare in the future. Imagine how you'd feel if you knew with certainty that your child required constant attention and care to survive—and the day might come that you weren't there to provide it. The future becomes a dark and scary place.

Parents in your church who have children with disabilities need to be reminded they can cling to God because he's always constant, never-changing, and omnipotent.

He's in charge of the future.

They aren't.

How are you helping families face the unknown with faith and confidence? And what help can you provide for interacting with all the agencies, medical facilities, and turmoil that comes with shuttling a child from appointment to appointment?

(continued from page 22)
of pestilence, famine, and disease. It's just a different place.

So you must go out and buy new guidebooks. And you must learn a whole new language. And you will meet a whole new group of people you would never have met.

It's just a different place. It's slower paced than Italy, less flashy than Italy. But after you've been there for a while and you catch your breath, you look around...and you begin to notice that Holland has windmills...and Holland has tulips. Holland even has Rembrandts.

But everyone you know is busy coming and going from Italy...and they're all bragging about what a wonderful time they had there. And for the rest of your life, you will say, "Yes, that's where I was supposed to go. That's what I had planned."

And the pain of that will never, ever, ever, ever go away...because the loss of that dream is a very, very significant loss.

But...if you spend your life mourning the fact that you didn't get to Italy, you may never be free to enjoy the very special, the very lovely things...about Holland.

We Needed to Have Our Child Build Relationships With Typically Developing Children

Many children with disabilities have few friends with whom they play outside of a school setting. This is sad not just for the special needs children but for the typical children as well.

Special needs children benefit from relationships because they'll become more socially competent. They'll try harder to do the same tasks as the typical children. And they'll be better prepared to live in the community.

Typical children benefit from exposure to special needs children by becoming more sensitive, patient, positive, and tolerant. They'll also have a more accurate view of individual differences. They're also provided with experiences with individuals who model success despite challenges.

Entering and sustaining play is one of the more difficult social accomplishments that typically developing children learn during their early years. A child with a disability will most likely need to learn to do this first by having a competent adult play partner. Having an adult close by will help the child know what to say and do when interacting with a typical child.

And that can't happen for Sarah without there being some typical children around willing to play and interact.

What Families Need: The Top Ten List

A group of parents whose children were diagnosed on the autism spectrum made a list of their top ten needs and concerns. They shared the list with me at a workshop:

10. Sleep (and the rest that comes with it)
9. Coping with family members' reactions
8. Coping with friends' reactions
7. Understanding what they did wrong to have disabled children
6. Wondering if they've done enough to help their children
5. Worrying about siblings not getting enough time or attention
4. Dealing with the effects on their marriage
3. Worrying about their children's future: Will their children have jobs?

special needs—special ministry
for children's ministry

2. Worrying about their children's future: Will their children be safe?

1. Worrying about their children's future: Who will love their children when the parents die?

Any parent can relate to some of the items on the list. Every parent has war stories about sleepless nights, embarrassing tantrums at the grocery store, sibling battles, and trips to the emergency room.

But parents of disabled children will probably experience those trials with greater intensity, and the trials will last longer. It's not uncommon for children with disabilities to experience insomnia on a regular basis or need medical intervention for months or even years at a time.

My friend's little girl has slept through the night just three times in four years. Another mother has two children with a food absorption disorder. Keeping them alive and healthy required her to give them medication through stomach feeding tubes every four hours, around the clock, throughout their infancy and early childhood years.

Look again at the list. Ask parents of disabled children if it strikes a chord and if they'd add something to the list.

You can't minister effectively to families who have disabled children until you *understand their lives;* these are the lives that these parents are living, day after day, week after week, perhaps forever.

Do you understand? Have you adapted your church's programming to be in sync with their daily lives?

Here's a glimpse of what it's like to be in a family that has a special needs child...

The demands are relentless.

When you live with a special needs child, developmental timetables are irrelevant. It's common for children who have disabilities to experience developmental delays in one or more areas. They may lag behind their peers physically, verbally, emotionally, and academically. This means that, even though the children experience development in the same predictable sequence as their nondisabled peers, their development occurs in slow motion.

Disabled children are typically more dependent on their parents for a longer period of time. Self-help skills such as dressing, bathing, and toileting may be significantly delayed.

Imagine for a moment doubling or tripling the time spent in every stage your child has gone through. Instead of changing diapers for two to three years, you buy and change diapers for four to six years. Instead of carrying your baby up and down stairs for ten to thirteen months, you carry your child for two to three years. The constant caregiving is physically and emotionally draining on the parents and other siblings in the home.

It's challenging for siblings.

Having a child with a disability usually means the balance of time and attention between children is extremely difficult to accomplish.

"It's just not fair" isn't a whiny complaint when applied to siblings in a family with a special needs child. It's an accurate statement.

The daily needs of a special needs child can easily overshadow the needs of a child developing typically. It's normal for the child who's most dependent to receive the lion's share of time and attention from parents…but it certainly isn't fair.

Scheduling extracurricular activities for the nondisabled children in a family can be a nightmare when added to the time and money spent taking a disabled brother or sister to and from therapy, doctor's appointments, and other related commitments. And if the disabled sibling has any behavior problems, even the most empathetic sibling can feel angry, embarrassed, or discouraged when the disabled child has an unpredictable meltdown in public.

Remember that the child with the disability isn't always the baby in the family. An older child with a disability who's aware of his or her limitations may be sad or resentful of the situation. And younger siblings may be embarrassed by the limitations of an older brother or sister.

Parents are stressed to the max.

Couples who have children with disabilities are at tremendous risk for separation and divorce.

There are money issues: The medical needs and ongoing therapy may quickly overwhelm the family budget.

Sometimes only one parent—usually the mother—is in charge of arranging and transporting the child to medical and therapy appointments. That can lead to feelings of resentment and isolation in *both* parents! The problem is further exacerbated if there's no extended family or friends to help with caregiving. Couples may have to rely on each other for a break, and that tag-team approach leaves little or no time alone to nurture their relationship.

And if you think you've been in an embarrassing situation with a typically developing child, imagine what it's like with a child who often experiences far more temper tantrums and louder and more frequent outbursts of misbehavior. Parents are constantly challenged to find ways of avoiding problem situations. It's an exhausting way to live.

If there's a family with a special needs child in your church, you can reduce their stress by providing very practical ministry that starts with listening. Friends who ask how our life is going and how they can pray for us help us feel we're not alone.

One couple, whose children were in Sarah's Sunday school class, even learned a few words in sign language when they heard Sarah was learning to communicate that way. It's a great feeling to have someone love your child who's not a paid professional.

> It's a great feeling to have someone love your child who's not a paid professional.

Baby sitters are lifesavers.

It's not easy for parents of typical children to find baby sitters. It's almost *impossible* for parents of special needs children to find baby sitters who can communicate with nonverbal children, feed children who are unable to feed themselves, or manage the behavior of an unpredictable child.

Parents of special needs children are still couples—and need time to invest in their marriage relationship. They need date nights. They need time away. Capable baby sitters are of immeasurable value. Even offering to watch the other siblings while mom or dad takes a special needs child to therapy can be a welcome relief.

Networking becomes essential.

There are times when it's helpful for parents of children with disabilities to talk to one another. Parents can share their experiences, feel understood, and develop a network of re-sources. Networks also provide a broader base of ideas for handling whatever situation families are facing.

Are you providing networking opportunities for parents?

And when it comes to church, here's what a special needs family needs…

We need unconditional love and acceptance.

God calls us to love each other in a way that's uncondi-tional—and rare. While I wish I could expect Sarah to receive unconditional love in the world, I can't. I *can* expect that she'll encounter it at church.

Why am I so sure? Because at church Sarah *gives* uncondi-tional love.

She's touched other lives with her smile and acceptance. I see it in the eyes and smiles of her Sunday school teachers when they welcome her into the children's worship hour. I see it when other parents greet her in the hallway between services. She's reaching out—and others are reaching back. Others who've looked be-yond Sarah's disability to see the child that God created.

Not every special needs child is able to reach out, to express love. Maybe you feel uncomfortable around kids who are dif-ferent. You're unsure what to do or say.

Here's what to do: Decide to walk in Jesus' steps. Decide to love—unconditionally.

We read that "I can do everything through him who gives me strength" (Philippians 4:13). But do you believe it? We read that "We know that in all things God works for the good of those who love him, who have been called according to his purpose" (Romans 8:28). But do you really believe it?

Look at my child through the eyes of God's love. That's what my family needs. That's what every family needs.

We need caring and informed Sunday school teachers.

Of course, I haven't always looked at special needs children the way I do now. I was trained to be an early childhood devel-opment specialist, an expert in *normal* child development.

I didn't want to teach "those" children. I didn't have a clue *how* to teach them. I felt uncomfortable around children with special needs. What would I say? What if I couldn't understand them? What if they didn't respond to me?

special needs—special ministry
for children's ministry

Parents of typical children usually find great programs for their kids at church. These parents can refuel with worship and teaching as their children learn with peers elsewhere in the building.

Not so for parents who bring their special needs child to church. These parents often feel vulnerable for themselves and for their child. It's difficult to encounter people who don't understand and who aren't always welcoming.

Plus, going to church is a break in the daily routine. That's not a problem with a typically developing child, but for a special needs child routines are a vital learning tool. Changing a special needs child's routine by taking him or her somewhere new or changing teachers at Sunday school can have devastating effects.

A new routine that's never been experienced, such as visiting a new church, can be *extremely* stressful. Parents may not be able to predict how their special needs child will react or how church members will react to their child. Something as simple as a large poster with pictures and simple labels that explain the order of the Sunday school hour can make a huge difference in the behavior of a child with special needs.

A Special Needs Family That Feels Understood at Church

I met Bill and Karen Freeman and their five-year-old daughter, Rebecca, through a Mothers of Preschoolers group. Rebecca was born with Down syndrome. Rebecca is now twelve. I asked Bill and Karen when, in their experience with churches, they've felt truly understood.

Here's what I heard...

"We felt understood when we felt refreshed."

To maintain a positive attitude during the ongoing challenge of caring for their disabled child, Bill and Karen needed fellowship and Bible study. When a teacher took charge of Rebecca so they could go to Sunday school together, they felt refreshed and their faith grew.

Another refreshing moment came when a friend supervised Rebecca for ten minutes so Bill and Karen could enjoy a short, meaningful conversation with a friend in the church's welcome center.

Are the parents of special needs children in your church experiencing spiritual refreshment? What can you do to help?

"We felt understood when we didn't have to do it all ourselves."

Bill and Karen did what many parents who have special needs children do: They took responsibility for activities that included their daughter. But after serving as Rebecca's Sunday school teacher, children's music leader, and Girl Scout leader, they discovered they were isolated from outlets and activities they needed as adults.

In addition, they were *tired*.

That's when Bill and Karen let go of the expectation they had to do it all. And they were relieved when other capable adults stepped in to fill those roles.

Is it your expectation that if a special needs child is involved in your program, a parent needs to be involved as well? Do parents of special needs children think that's the case?

"We felt understood when church staff communicated with us about our daughter."

For Bill and Karen, it was a relief knowing the church staff understood Rebecca's needs, challenges, and strengths.

Each new school year presented the same challenge: What class should she be in? Who would help her? Was the social contact important enough to keep her with children her age? Was this the best place for her to learn what is important for her spiritual growth?

Bill and Karen coached teachers and helpers until Bill and Karen were comfortable enough to leave Rebecca in their care. But church staff and volunteers change frequently, so communication sometimes faltered.

And when a church didn't understand Rebecca or have the resources to help, Bill and Karen moved to a church that *did* communicate and have resources. The cost of not making a move was letting Rebecca slip through the cracks. For any parent, that's an unacceptable cost.

How are you communicating with parents of special needs children in your church?

"We felt understood when church programs made room for Rebecca."

Rebecca has participated in vacation Bible school, children's chorus, summer music camp, and Sunday school. Because those programs highlighted drama and music as teaching mediums, Rebecca could participate and function well. Those are settings in which she flourishes.

Rebecca was also welcomed to join group activities because church leaders provided parental involvement and adaptive assistance.

Which of your children's ministry programs are *truly* open to children with special needs?

"We felt understood when Rebecca was able to do ministry as well as receive it."

Bill and Karen are pleased that their church understands and allows Rebecca to assist in the Sunday preschool ministry as a teacher's helper. Their daughter is able to be a fully functioning, giving member of Christ's body.

And that glorifies God in amazing ways.

Just for You

It's easy to think of a special needs ministry for children as just that—for children.

But that's not true. It also blesses parents and siblings. It provides precious space for a married couple to enjoy a cup of coffee together or to worship together. It lets a tired mommy take her typical child to the mall for some one-on-one time that won't be interrupted.

You're reaching out to children, but your loving touch reaches others, too. What an impact you're having in families' lives!

Dear God,

Thank you that serving you is often like dropping a stone in a quiet lake — the ripples stretch out and reach far beyond our expectations. Bless the families of the children our ministry serves.

In Jesus' name, amen.

3. The Special Needs Ministry Launch Countdown Checklist

by Pat Verbal

You're thinking of launching a special needs ministry or expanding the ministry already underway in your church.

Before you take that next step, here's a quick checklist of four things to do now.

☑ *Check your church culture.*

A few years ago the Oldsmobile company tried to pull itself out of a sales slump with the slogan, "It's not your father's Oldsmobile."

The campaign was a flop. It failed to put young singles in oversized cars, and within a few years General Motors closed down their Oldsmobile division. The slogan went on to be mocked on late-night talk shows and become the punch line in plenty of jokes.

The problem was that Oldsmobiles—large, domestic cars—*were* the sort of car your father drove. They were big, heavy, and could haul a family of five on vacation. *Saying* they were different didn't *make* them different. Young drivers looked at the people who were actually driving Oldsmobiles and saw people who looked *exactly* like their fathers.

The campaign failed because most people believe their own ideas before they believe what others tell them. A clever slogan can't change a deeply held prejudice against Oldsmobiles—or anything else.

I think the same principle applies to people with special needs. Our culture has created a prejudice against them.

How many positive portrayals have you seen of people with special needs on television or in a movie? Probably very few, if any. The world looks at people with special needs and thinks "damaged goods." These people don't fit the culture's notion of heroes, no matter how loving or caring they may be.

Now think about how many people with disabilities fill places of ministry and leadership in a typical local church. Not many. Could that be because Christians have adopted the world's view of people with disabilities rather than a biblical view?

The first step in establishing a special needs ministry is to determine what your church thinks of people with disabilities. *Are* they damaged goods? Or are they something else?

Just asking the question won't necessarily get you an honest answer. Few people will risk being politically incorrect by saying, "Well, yes, I really don't see a place for a child with Down syndrome here."

The way to tell if your church's culture is open to people with disabilities is to evaluate what your church *does,* not what your leadership *says.* Check the fruit of your ministry.

How to Determine the Way Your Church *Really* Feels About People With Special Needs

That your church doesn't have a special needs ministry in place doesn't make you a terrible congregation. Far from it.

According to Dr. James Dobson, the church as a whole is not meeting the needs of the disabled. *Most* churches don't have programs that include the deaf, the disabled, or those with special needs—though there are exceptions.

In a broadcast titled "Mothers of Handicapped Children," Dr. Dobson pointed out the obvious: When people who have special needs come to church and realize there's no one like themselves there, they leave—and never come back.

Said Dr. Dobson, "I really feel that the Christian church is going to have to examine its values at this point, because there but for the grace of God go I or my child."

Like Dr. Dobson, most Christians readily agree that special needs ministry is important. They express great appreciation for people who serve in this area. So what's the problem? Why aren't there more ministries up and running?

I think the problem comes when churches try to identify their role in reaching families who don't fit into the church's traditional programs. The notion of launching new programs strikes fear in the hearts of church staff. Who will oversee them? fund them? staff them? When it's a major problem trying to get enough Sunday school teachers, how can the church even *think* of creating a new class or program?

Often a desire to start a special needs ministry dies right there on the launching pad—shot down before it's even attempted. Yet your church believes that children with special needs must be given an opportunity to hear and respond to the good news. Nobody is voting against the notion that God can use people with special needs.

Do this: Determine what your church truly believes by using the following assessment tool. Place a mark on the chart that reflects what you're doing—not what you're saying—on this Action Assessment Line. The tool is adapted from one created by Dr. Scott Daniels and Dr. Steve Green.

Action Assessment Line

Conviction   Value   Ownership   Action

☑ **Conviction** is the belief that something should be done by someone but not necessarily by your church. Your church is probably here if your leadership responds to your questions about launching a special needs ministry with lots of agreement that "It's a great idea and something we should definitely put on a future agenda for discussion and exploration." It's *especially* true if you have children with special needs in your church already—but there's no programming to meet their needs.

☑ **Value** is the next step toward taking action. It's recognizing that the "good idea" actually connects to part of the church's mission statement, that it reflects the church's values, and that being intentional about serving families who have special needs children might fit into a vision for sharing the gospel with your community. If the response of your church leadership is along the lines of "We can see how that

special needs—special ministry
for children's ministry

would help us accomplish our mission," then place a mark on "value."

☑ **Ownership** happens when there are people in your church who already have responsibility for this sort of ministry. Typically special needs ministries enter a church through the children's ministry, but not always. If your leadership says, "That sounds like something Nancy should be handling," then you're in the orbit of ownership.

Of course, if Nancy is an already-overworked, part-time children's pastor who has no idea where to begin with a special needs ministry, ownership may be a mirage. Until someone looks you in the eye, and says, "I'll do it," or gives you permission to move ahead yourself, you don't have authentic ownership.

☑ **Action** occurs when you actually begin shaping your church's special needs ministry. Your church leadership has given you its blessing—or at least its permission—to start. You have a budget, though it may be humble. You have the opportunity to report back to the leadership what you're doing, why you're doing it, and what you hope to accomplish.

You know you've finally arrived at the action step when you can put something about a special needs ministry in the church bulletin, and you aren't asked by your pastor what you're up to.

What is your church's culture regarding special needs ministry? Where did you place a mark on the line? It's good to know where you are because that's your starting point.

Your goal is to move your church leadership from the conviction end of the Action Assessment Line toward the action end. *That's* where things happen.

You have three tools at your disposal:

1. Prayer

Nothing can substitute for you spending time in prayer. Pray for your church leadership and your willingness to be sensitive to God's timing. Pray for the families the ministry can reach. Pray for staff and volunteers to emerge. Pray for your own motives and the motives of your ministry. Pray for grace, patience, and love.

2. Passion

It's been said nothing happens in the church until there's a zealot who's willing to make it happen. There's some truth in that statement, though it's also true that zealots need to quickly make friends who'll help shoulder the load. Are you that zealot? Are there people willing to help you?

The need for caring volunteers who'll take a ministry and run with it is huge for church leaders. It's one thing for you to meet with your pastor and say, "Someone really ought to do something." It's another thing to add, "And I'm that someone."

Are you that someone?

3. Education

A well-known Christian leader has recently begun to speak out on behalf of special needs ministries in the church. Though this leader has had a platform for years from which he could shine a spotlight on this need, it's never been something he actively, publicly supported.

Then he had a grandchild who is a special needs child. That reality has educated him on the importance of the church welcoming special needs children. It's made the issue significant to him in a way it wasn't before.

I don't question the compassion of this leader—he's demonstrated tremendous compassion. And a willingness to do ministry. That's not my point.

I simply mean that when we're faced personally with an issue, it comes into focus quickly and rapidly moves up our list of priorities. In the same way that stubbing your toe reminds you that your toes have been faithfully serving you for weeks without you giving them any thought, so does having a real, live person enter your building in a wheelchair remind you that a special needs ministry is important.

Suddenly a vague belief that your church should think through how to minister to those with special needs gets big-time attention.

You can educate your church leadership several ways. Here are some suggestions:

You can provide literature and statistics. Some leaders want to know the numbers. Why is this ministry more important to fund than another one? What do you intend to do? Chapter 5 will help you think through how to approach leaders like this.

You can take them on a field trip. What church in your area is already doing a special needs ministry? Go on a "snoop trip" where you get a tour, meet some of the teachers and leaders, and hear firsthand what the benefits are for the church.

You can bring someone with you. If you've got fifteen minutes to present your case to your pastor or a church board, why not bring a family that has a special needs child with you? Ask the family to take half the time explaining what they need, and you take the rest of the time describing a program that would meet those needs.

You can provide a dose of reality. Invite a family with a special needs child to evaluate your existing program. Share that family's evaluation with your leaders. It's very possible your church leadership doesn't have a clue how your programs work—or don't work—for special needs families. We all like to know how we're doing; if you flunk the evaluation, say so and offer your suggestions for how to pass it the next time.

> Invite a family with a special needs child to evaluate your existing program.

How you educate your leaders depends on who they are—and how they learn. But it's generally true that you'll see little change until you demonstrate there's a real need, and your leaders discover that need. A PowerPoint presentation will never be as effective as providing an emotional connection with living, breathing children and families who want to see a program happen.

☑ Check your motives.

What's your personal view of children with special needs?

I ask that question because it gets to motivation. If you're motivated by pity, your ministry will be short lived. You won't have the passion or vision to see it through.

If you're motivated by guilt, you'll run out of steam even more quickly. Why? Because once you've pulled together a program, your guilt will be gone. And with it will go your motivation to work through all the logistics and issues that surround special needs ministry.

If you're motivated by the need your own child has for appropriate programming—if you're the parent of a special needs child—recognize that you'll probably be involved for a limited amount of time. When your child moves into another group, you'll most likely leave the ministry. God can still use you while you're here in a powerful way, but be mindful to build a strong leadership team who can carry on when you leave.

About the only motivation that will sustain you long term is love. Love for children. Love for their families. Love for sharing the gospel. Love for serving others.

And along with motivation, there's another question to ask yourself and others who might join you in a special needs ministry. It's this: What do *you* think about people with special needs?

Thomas Orrin Bentz, author of *Theology in Disability*, believes Christians are nearsighted regarding special needs ministry. He writes, "Theology not only deals with disability. Theology is disability. It is the impossible science of the supernatural, the search for the 'law of God,' the knowing of the unknowable, trying to see the infinite through our nearsighted lenses."

Here's my point: God's image is sometimes revealed in twenty perfect, little fingers and toes. At other times, it's seen in tiny, twisted limbs and bright, crooked smiles. Babies born with physical limitations aren't a mistake of nature—they're a new means of approaching grace.

Do you believe that God can be in the creation of a child who's born without the ability to ever walk? or speak? or move cognitively past an ability to experience the world in concrete terms?

Like all children, children with special needs want to know they have value and purpose. They're limited, but not without potential. The world may abort them or shut them away; some churches may marginalize them. But God lifts them to places of honor. As we work with children with special needs, we *must* think of them as full brothers and sisters in the Lord, not people who are less than us.

☑ Check your vision.

People don't jump in and help programs; they help people. And they don't sign on for programs that seem to have a small impact.

Be sure you connect your vision for a special needs program with the larger mission and purpose of your church.

Is your church missions minded? Present your ministry as a mission outreach to a population of people who often don't find a place in the church because the church doesn't reach out to them.

Is your church outreach oriented? Present your ministry as just that: an outreach program that will meet critical needs in the community.

Is your church one that values following the example of Christ? You couldn't find a ministry that more closely shows Christ's heart for people.

special needs—special ministry
for children's ministry

Jesus' Heart for People With Special Needs

There's nothing in how Jesus responded to people with disabilities that indicates he esteemed them any less than the healthy crowds that surrounded him. Reading through the Gospels, it's easy to see that Jesus didn't turn away the disabled, ridicule them, or suggest they were incapable of discipleship and service.

Consider the way Jesus responded to these people with disabilities...

- He welcomed and healed the lepers, the sickest of the sick and the likely most disfigured (Matthew 8:1-4; Luke 17:11-19).
- He gave his undivided attention to the deaf-mute, then touched and healed him (Mark 7:31-37).
- He gave purpose, hope, and healing to a blind man (John 9:1-41).
- In the presence of religious persecution, he healed a man's crippled hand (Luke 6:6-11).

Jesus engaged people with disabilities. He touched them, spoke with them, ministered to them. He had a vision for them that didn't rely on their being whole and healed before they had value.

Jesus *did* heal people—but he didn't heal everyone with disabilities. There were certainly people in Jerusalem who were still lame when Jesus ended his ministry on earth. Jesus could have simply waved a hand and healed every leper on earth—but he didn't. He could have restored sight to all unseeing eyes, prayed strength into all bent, twisted legs and ankles—but he didn't.

Why not? He had the power, and he certainly had the compassion.

Perhaps it's because from an eternal perspective what matters more is the condition of the heart, not how well someone can walk.

Kathleen Deyer Bolduc writes this regarding her son's disability: "The pain I experienced as I grieved Joel's disability broke open the Scriptures for me. I came to understand that Jesus turns upside down the cultural belief that brokenness is to be avoided at all costs. Christ challenged me to face and embrace my brokenness as well as Joel's brokenness, so that God's power might be released within both of us."

Of the miracles Jesus performed in the Gospels, nearly two-thirds were done to assist people who had physical needs. As hurting people cried out to Jesus, he responded compassionately. And he's still responding—through us.

Jesus had a deep, unceasing affection for hurting people. Twelve times the Bible says he was "moved by compassion" or he had "compassion on them." He also honored the faith of family and friends who brought their suffering loved ones to him. Jesus never drew back in revulsion at the sight of a person who had special needs. He never shook his head and referred them to a clinic or center for help. He saw no hopeless cases. Jesus' vision for the disabled didn't include them being less valuable because of their special needs. Prayerfully consider the compassion and respect Jesus demonstrated in the following passages.

Mark 1:40-45

A man with leprosy came to him and begged him on his knees, "If you are willing, you can make me clean."

Filled with compassion, Jesus reached out his hand and touched the man. "I am willing," he said. "Be clean!" Immediately the leprosy left him and he was cured.

Jesus sent him away at once with a strong warning: "See that you don't tell this to anyone. But go, show yourself to the priest and offer the sacrifices that Moses commanded for your cleansing, as a testimony to them." Instead he went out and began to talk freely, spreading the news. As a result, Jesus could no longer enter a town openly but stayed outside in lonely places. Yet the people still came to him from everywhere.

Luke 5:17-26

One day as he was teaching, Pharisees and teachers of the law, who had come from every village of Galilee and from Judea and Jerusalem, were sitting there. And the power of the Lord was present for him to heal the sick. Some men came carrying a paralytic on a mat and tried to take him into the house to lay him before Jesus. When they could not find a way to do this because of the crowd, they went up on the roof and lowered him on his mat through the tiles into the middle of the crowd, right in front of Jesus.

When Jesus saw their faith, he said, "Friend, your sins are forgiven."

The Pharisees and the teachers of the law began thinking to themselves, "Who is this fellow who speaks blasphemy? Who can forgive sins but God alone?"

Jesus knew what they were thinking and asked, "Why are you thinking these things in your hearts? Which is easier: to say, 'Your

sins are forgiven,' or to say, 'Get up and walk'? But that you may know that the Son of Man has authority on earth to forgive sins..." He said to the paralyzed man, "I tell you, get up, take your mat and go home." Immediately he stood up in front of them, took what he had been lying on and went home praising God. Everyone was amazed and gave praise to God. They were filled with awe and said, "We have seen remarkable things today."

John 5:1-9

Some time later, Jesus went up to Jerusalem for a feast of the Jews. Now there is in Jerusalem near the Sheep Gate a pool, which in Aramaic is called Bethesda and which is surrounded by five covered colonnades. Here a great number of disabled people used to lie — the blind, the lame, the paralyzed. One who was there had been an invalid for thirty-eight years. When Jesus saw him lying there and learned that he had been in this condition for a long time, he asked him, "Do you want to get well?"

"Sir," the invalid replied, "I have no one to help me into the pool when the water is stirred. While I am trying to get in, someone else goes down ahead of me."

Then Jesus said to him, "Get up! Pick up your mat and walk." At once the man was cured; he picked up his mat and walked.

Mark 8:22-26

They came to Bethsaida, and some people brought a blind man and begged Jesus to touch him. He took the blind man by the hand and led him outside the village. When he had spit on the man's eyes and put his hands on him, Jesus asked, "Do you see anything?"

He looked up and said, "I see people; they look like trees walking around."

Once more Jesus put his hands on the man's eyes. Then his eyes were opened, his sight was restored, and he saw everything clearly. Jesus sent him home, saying, "Don't go into the village."

Matthew 9:1-8

Jesus stepped into a boat, crossed over and came to his own town. Some men brought to him a paralytic, lying on a mat. When Jesus saw their faith, he said to the paralytic, "Take heart, son; your sins are forgiven."

At this, some of the teachers of the law said to themselves, "This fellow is blaspheming!"

Knowing their thoughts, Jesus said, "Why do you entertain evil thoughts in your hearts? Which is easier: to say, 'Your sins are forgiven,' or to say, 'Get up and walk'? But so that you may know that the Son of Man has authority on earth to forgive sins… " Then he said to the paralytic, "Get up, take your mat and go home." And the man got up and went home. When the crowd saw this, they were filled with awe; and they praised God, who had given such authority to men.

Does Your Vision Reflect Jesus' Vision?

Jesus never excluded or marginalized the special needs community. Decide now what vision *you'll* communicate about serving the special needs community. Think through how that vision will be heard by your church leadership and the congregation at large. Determine the ways that a special needs ministry will advance the goals and mission of your church.

You must be able to communicate your vision clearly and powerfully. It's essential if you're going to build an effective ministry.

☑ Check to see what's stopping you.

What are the obstacles standing in your way? Maybe it's a lack of time, an uncertainty about exactly what to do next, or a desire to see if anyone else will get involved and take the reins.

The Action Assessment Line introduced earlier might give you some powerful clues and insights as to what's stopping your church from embracing a special needs ministry. How well are you moving from conviction to value to ownership to action? What's stopping the process may be a lack of understanding or a perceived lack of resources.

I'll tell you what it isn't—it *isn't* a lack of caring. I've yet to meet a pastor who wants to deliberately keep special needs families away from church. I've yet to meet a children's pastor who truly wants children with ADD to stay home on Sunday morning watching cartoons.

The make-or-break challenge is usually that there's simply no energy to make a special needs ministry happen.

Ellen, a children's pastor in Oregon, told me, "We don't have a special needs ministry because I can't keep up with all I have to do now. I have 250 children and eighty teachers every Sunday morning. I have to make sure everything is up and running, and our classrooms are overcrowded."

Leaders like Ellen are exhausted. "I get paid for thirty hours a week and work fifty. I'm a single mom with four kids. I make sixty phone calls a month to get volunteers. One Sunday I taught in Trevor's classroom. He has autism and I had to bolt the door just to keep him from running down the hall. It's a big job to work with Trevor, and volunteers are not prepared. I'd love to do more, but it's impossible to add one more thing."

Ellen's right: There's always one more thing to do in children's ministry. The job is never really finished.

Are you the person to launch or expand the special needs ministry at your church? Or you might be the one who will put this book into the hands of the person who *is* the right person. One or the other, I hope so.

> "I'd love to do more, but it's impossible to add one more thing."

Moving ahead can literally redeem lives. It will almost certainly improve them. Consider what I discovered when I talked with LuAnn Ruoss, Director of the Special Needs Ministry at First Presbyterian Church in Bakersfield, California. She shared some harsh realities about life as a person with special needs.

Pat: LuAnn, you see young people who are developmentally delayed trying to live on their own. What challenges do they face?

LuAnn: Many of them try to get menial jobs to supplement their Social Security checks. They're taught life skills to help them handle money, hygiene, and household duties. Some live together in apartments and others in group homes. Because they are free to come and go as they choose, it's easy for them to become overwhelmed with too many choices.

Pat: That sounds exciting but a little scary, too. Do most of them succeed?

LuAnn: Success for these young people is difficult, especially in relationships. The state tells them that they can make choices to use condoms or not during sexual relations. The state *doesn't* teach them about abstinence. Sometimes they make friends with people who abuse them and take advantage of their mental capacity.

Pat: That's terrible. Does it happen a lot?

LuAnn: I'm afraid it does. At the beginning of the month, when paychecks are mailed out, they have lots of friends. Some drink and party together until the money runs out. Friends without disabilities tell sad stories and ask for money. One girl made a friend's car payment because the friend let her ride in the car. In the end, adults with special needs are very lonely.

Pat: It sounds more like abuse than friendship. Can't something be done about that?

LuAnn: It's clearly abuse. The disabled are often victimized and become very untrusting of people in general.

Pat: Is that when they turn to the church?

LuAnn: Sadly, at church many of them are not invited to be part of the group. My heart goes out to them because instead of breaking the long cycle of loneliness, churches add to their confusion.

Pat: How is it different at your church?

LuAnn: We intentionally reach out to people of all ages. Developmentally delayed adults go to Sunday school classes and are welcomed into membership. They serve as ushers and greeters. I visit group homes and connect them with the regional center for the disabled and Heart Connection, a support group sponsored by our church. We offer a conference locally that trains our church members to understand the needs of these precious young adults.

Pat: Can you share some success stories?

LuAnn: I love to talk about my friends.

David, a forty-year-old man with severe learning disabilities, was raised in church. For many years he could not work full time and was not involved in church. When David joined our ministry, we began giving him leadership roles that challenged him. As a result, he started work on his associate arts degree and secured a full-time job counseling others with disabilities at a community center. David went from a part-time dishwasher to a Bible study leader who enjoys going to Promise Keepers with the men in our church.

Mary suffered with mental illness for years. With lots of love, Mary slowly changed from someone who didn't feel safe at Sunday school to a mentor for new members in her class. Now, instead of just sitting quietly, Mary freely participates when asked. It's a joy watching her grow in the Lord.

When I first started our special needs class five years ago, Robert was part of the original group. He had attended church since he was a teenager, but he wouldn't pray out loud. As his relationship grew with God and others, his mom's health began to deteriorate. Robert requested prayer for her, but didn't pray for three years. He said he didn't know how. Imagine our surprise when one day Robert volunteered to lead prayer time and simply began talking to God. I know God listens to Robert and answers his prayers.

Pat: What do you teach people with limited understanding about God?

LuAnn: It's too easy to say that people with mental disabilities will all go to heaven, so there's no need to worry about what they understand. I've watched them come to a personal knowledge of Jesus Christ.

One spring I asked my class what Easter meant to them. They talked about new clothes, candy, and going out to dinner. The next year my husband and I created a hands-on lesson to teach the Easter story. We brought in blocks of wood and different sized nails. They loved pounding

special needs—special ministry
for children's ministry

the nails into the blocks and making a lot of noise. Then we brought in a wooden cross and three huge spikes. As they started swinging their hammers, Joe stopped.

He said, "Is that the sound Jesus heard when they nailed him to the cross?" I nodded my head yes. All the color drained from Joe's face.

He put down his hammer and tried to push the nails in with his hands. The harsh sounds stopped as other students followed his lead. Soon the room was quiet. Finally, the message was real for them. Now when you ask them about Easter, they talk about how Jesus Christ died for them.

We want to help you find the support you need and help you train the workers who'll make your ministry happen.

Dr. Jim Pierson has been fighting the good fight for establishing special needs ministries for more than thirty years. In Chapter 5, you'll find his advice on how to take your request to launch a special needs ministry to your church leadership.

But before you continue reading, pause for a moment and reflect on the "Just for You" devotion below. You're stepping forward to do important work for the kingdom—it's important you do so prayerfully.

Just for You

When the four friends brought their crippled friend to Jesus, they ran into obstacles. The crowd was too thick. The doorway was blocked. They couldn't get in.

But they wouldn't be stopped. They carried their friend to the roof and created a skylight that the homeowner certainly didn't approve of. And their friend was able to get to Jesus.

You're one of those special friends. You're helping carve a path for special needs friends in your community to make their way to church— toward fellowship and toward Jesus.

God bless you for your compassion, energy, and love.

Dear God,

Bless the journey of our church's special needs ministry. In all ways, at all times, we ask you to provide the guidance we need.

In Jesus' name, amen.

4. Case Studies: Special Needs Ministries in Real Churches

by Louise Tucker Jones

As I speak with special ministries directors across the country, I'm *amazed* at the creative ways they build their ministries. Each ministry takes on a unique design, shaped to meet the needs of a particular area or church.

I applaud all efforts to minister to individuals with disabilities. I recently heard a report on the radio that said only *5 percent* of churches provide programming for this population of people. I believe that percentage.

Following are programs that are making a difference in local churches. Perhaps the program you have—or will be launching—resembles one of them.

How Do Special Needs Ministries Look in a Local Church?

Sue Lindahl, who has a background in special education and was a missionary, is not only the director of the special ministries department at Stonebriar Community Church in Frisco, Texas, but is also a part-time staff member. This lends great credibility when presenting needs at staff meetings.

Now in its fourth year, the program emphasizes inclusion and serves birth through high school. Each child is given a *buddy* to help in the regular classroom. And for those medically fragile children who can't attend a regular class, Sue has two classrooms available, along with on-call nurses and volunteers.

"Our philosophy is 'one child at a time,' and we do what it takes to meet each child's needs," says Sue. The church also offers a one-night-a-month respite program called Fun Zone for special needs students attending their church, along with their siblings. Volunteers are seldom hard to find. Sue has high standards and finds that the more she expects from her volunteers, the more motivated people are to be involved.

Harvest Bible Chapel in Rolling Meadows, Illinois, has a membership of more than six thousand people with three worship services. They also have two distinct special needs ministries. The first ministry reaches out to deaf and hearing impaired individuals. *Signing* is a part of the second worship service, and classes in American Sign Language are offered regularly to people in the church so that they may communicate with the deaf community.

The second ministry, In His Image, is a program designed for adults with special needs. Twenty individuals enjoy the opening and music of the third worship service and then attend a Bible study program geared especially for their needs. Children with special needs are mainstreamed weekly into regular classrooms with one-on-one aides.

These are just a few examples of creative special needs ministries. Remember that each ministry will look different depending on whom it's designed to serve and how far it's grown.

Birthing a Ministry

Second Baptist Church in Houston, Texas, is just beginning a special needs ministry program called Promise Land, which is geared to first through fifth grades. Children go to a regular Bible study group the first hour and then attend Promise Land during the worship time. During Promise Land, children are exposed to teaching that includes lots of tactile stimulation. Wendee Garnett says that during this first year, Promise Land is constantly being adapted to meet needs.

Rachel Richardson is a nineteen-year-old college student. When she started volunteering in the special needs program at Quail Springs Church of Christ, there were just three students. But suddenly Rachel found herself responsible for the entire ministry.

When the teacher left, Rachel was appointed special ministry director and told, "Do what you want to do." After the initial shock, Rachel got on the phone and called every resource person she could find to help her establish a program. She's even attending conferences while carrying a full-time class schedule at the university. "I'm overwhelmed," says Rachel, "but I really want to make this program work. I love these kids."

Rachel was tossed in the deep end of the pool, while Wendee waded in gradually. Special needs ministries are birthed in both ways.

Building a Ministry

For twenty years Ethel Evans taught special education in the public schools. She now serves as director of the special ministry program at First Baptist in Moore, Oklahoma.

Twelve years ago Ethel volunteered to help with the church's special ministry program that had two children and one teacher. When that teacher left, Ethel was the lone teacher of four students, consisting of both adults and children.

The following year a couple joined the teaching ranks, and ten years later the church's five teachers serve six children and six adults in a Bible study program. And though Ethel is now directing rather than teaching, she still leads the extended session for students who can't go into worship service. "I think our children need the consistency that one person offers," says Ethel. "They need to know that person will always be there and take care of their needs."

Both children and adult groups can participate in a program called Special Friends.

The adult special needs students who attend First Baptist all live at home rather than in group facilities and have either medical problems or disabilities so severe that they're unable to work in the community. They must have caregivers twenty-four hours a day. Because of this, the church developed a respite program which allows adult students to come to the church from ten in the morning to two in the afternoon the first and third Thursday of each month. While at respite, volunteers assist as students sing, listen to a guest singer, have a Bible study, enjoy fun activities, and eat lunch.

The children's program offers an AWANA class on Sunday evenings, and both children and adult groups can participate in a program called Special Friends. Every Christmas and Easter, students create cards the church mails to a local women's correctional facility. "It's a way for them to minister to others," says Ethel.

Though the church's ministry is small, it's consistent—and growing. The church has found unique ways to minister to challenged individuals, always with the goal of communicating that Jesus loves each student unconditionally.

A Blossoming Ministry

The Williams Boulevard Baptist Church in Kenner, Louisiana, has a special ministry program that serves 175 adult students and also ministers to fifty group-home staff members who attend with the students. Fifteen church members, including a nurse, teach the Sunday classes.

You might think those numbers reflect a mega-church, but Williams Boulevard has a membership of just nine hundred people. "At least 98 percent of the membership embrace our students," says director Cindy Mazza, who began the ministry twenty-seven years ago with two children. Cindy chuckles when asked how the ministry has grown so large.

"We had two families with special needs children, so we visited each family and asked for one name of another family," says Cindy. The church then went to the families whose names had been provided and asked for *another* name. A ministry was born.

> Cindy chuckles when asked how the ministry has grown so large.

When local schools started inclusion, so did the church. All their special needs children are now in regular classrooms. The adult student population grew dramatically when the state of Louisiana closed institutions nearby, and many adults with special needs were absorbed into group homes in the area.

Thankfully, the church was ready for the influx of new students. Already ministering to more than fifty adults, many coming from a community home in the area, the church simply moved from classrooms to the gymnasium when the attendance exploded.

"You would think we would have a multitude of small classes," says Cindy, "but the students like to be with each other, so we actually have only two separate classes." One class is a more advanced Bible study for those who have a higher level of understanding, and the other class presents the Bible story in a more tangible fashion with drama, puppets, flannel graph, and one-on-one help. But everyone comes together for music, the students' favorite activity.

Because of their love for music, at Christmas and the Fourth of July the students sing at nursing homes. "They need to give back to the community," says Cindy, "and this is an excellent way to do so."

Other activities include a September picnic; Christmas party; bowling after church; lunch at the church with recreation activities in the gym; and a special ministry day in October, when the group sings for the whole church. When the group was smaller, group members once rented trolleys and picnicked while they toured New Orleans.

The church also has special pancake breakfasts to honor the staff that come with students. "We see the staff as a ministry as much as the students," says Cindy. Many of the staff have never gone to church, so Sunday morning can be an outreach to them as well as the students.

Create a Place for Everyone

I once visited with a pastor and asked if his church had a ministry to people with special needs. His words were surprising, yet typical. He said, "No, because we don't have anyone with disabilities in our church." Of *course* he had no people with disabilities in his church—his church wasn't accessible to them physically or spiritually. I marvel at such a mind-set.

> Of *course* he had no people with disabilities in his church—his church wasn't accessible to them physically or spiritually.

Would we ever plant a new church without providing a children's program? Of course not, even if the people planting the church didn't have children. We'd have a program ready, waiting expectantly for that first family with little ones to walk through the front door.

Let's be just as zealous in providing for families with special needs. No one should be turned away from God's house; nor should we have to scramble around and offer a quick, inadequate, makeshift program because nothing is in place when the family arrives.

A friend of mine once took her son with Williams syndrome to a new church and explained Brian's disability to the children's director. My friend wanted her son placed in an appropriate Sunday school class. Surprisingly, the director requested that they not attend Sunday school that particular morning. "Let me work on this and find the right class, then I'll call you," she said.

My friend waited for a call that never came.

Each Sunday morning as the other children filed out of the auditorium for Sunday school, Brian would turn to his mom with a disheartened look and say, "I can't go, can I?" Oh, how it breaks my heart to see one of God's precious gems wounded by superficial Christianity.

We should be prepared to minister to anyone who walks through our church doors, *especially* to people with special needs. The world is often a painful and lonely place for them. Churches like those I've described demonstrate that your church can be the refuge they need. Let's eagerly accept these families and children with open arms—and the love of Jesus.

5. First Steps for Launching a Children's Special Needs Ministry

by Jim Pierson

A couple asked me to join them as an advocate for their son at a meeting with school officials. A tense discussion about new goals for the boy's education plan had reached an impasse. Perhaps to relieve tension, the principal asked the child's father, "What's the main goal you want your son to attain?"

Because of the nature of the conversation to that point, we expected the reply: "Relate appropriately with his peers"; or perhaps, "Read at age level."

He answered from his heart: "I want my son to know who Jesus is."

The young dad's response represents the feelings of lots of families. Christian parents want their children with disabilities to develop spiritually as well as intellectually, physically, and socially. Because of a federal mandate to educate children in the mainstream, families are accustomed to having their children included with their age mates in neighborhood schools. That's what's normal.

I believe parents should also expect children with special needs to be educated in the mainstream of their church's education program. The basic objective of your special needs ministry should be to include students with special needs in the *existing* classes in Sunday school, children's church, and other programs. Other ministry facets can be added as your program grows, such as ministry to families, ministry to siblings, and ministry to agencies serving the disability community.

You're on the front lines.

Children's pastors are often the first members of a church staff to encounter children with special needs and their families. It's people like you, people who are serving children, who sense the need. Who see it up close and personal. You're challenged by the opportunity to do ministry.

The purpose of this chapter is to give you information that helps you include children with disabilities in the various children's ministry programs that already exist in your church.

You can do it—and you can do it right.

Start with a meeting.

To start the process, ask for a meeting to discuss the rationale for the ministry and to lay the groundwork. For many years, I've done workshops and seminars for children's pastors to help them develop such ministries. I've learned what issues concern them and what issues concern their church leadership. It helps if you begin with a meeting in which the agenda addresses those issues.

Ask for a meeting to discuss the rationale for the ministry and to lay the groundwork.

But before you schedule your initial meeting, consider who should attend the meeting. I'd suggest this as a core group: your senior pastor, the board member responsible for children's ministry, a parent of a child with a disability, a parent of a typical child, the minister in charge of adult education, the youth pastor, a professional in the congregation who works with people with disabilities (if there is one), and an adult with a disability.

To get a positive outcome from the meeting, I suggest you include the topics I've listed below. They're hot buttons for the people I've suggested you invite. It will reassure the people you've gathered if you demonstrate you've thought about the issues that impact their areas of ministry.

Meeting agenda:

- Open with prayer for God's wisdom and direction.
- Read Psalm 139:13 and affirm the God-designed value of people with disabilities.
- Share your plan to involve the leadership of your church.
- Communicate your vision and plan for a disabilities ministry.

special needs—special ministry
for children's ministry

- Share how you'll find the people with disabilities in your congregation.
- Define and communicate your ministry model. Emphasize inclusion, which will dramatically reduce the need for space, budget, and materials.
- Address how you'll provide staff training.
- Describe your plan for controlling behavior—in advance.
- Describe how you'll communicate with families experiencing disabilities—and families that aren't.
- Identify places for church members with disabilities to serve in your congregation.
- Share your plan for transitioning students through the teen and adult departments of your church.
- Describe the rewards your church will experience because you have a disability ministry.

Quite an agenda! Here's some advice about how to move ahead in each of the areas listed above.

Pray for God's wisdom and direction.

Keep the planning, your children and their families, and your current and future volunteers surrounded in prayer. As you embark on sharing Jesus' love with children with special needs, ask their Creator to bless your efforts.

Organize a prayer team. Assign these segments of the ministry to specific members of your team for prayer: teachers, volunteers, parents, and children. Be sure everyone in the ministry is being regularly prayed for by someone else.

When it comes to praying for each child, ask the family for permission to share the child's needs with the person who is praying for the child...and to share the family's needs as well. Pray that children's involvement will help them realize their God-given potential. Pray that children will hear the message of God's love and respond to it. Pray that families' needs will be met, both physically and spiritually.

Pray for your volunteers. Pray that children without disabilities will enjoy their friends with disabilities. Pray that your congregation will embrace this ministry. Occasionally send notes to remind people that they're being lifted up in prayer.

Recognize the value of every person.

Recognize the value of every person regardless of disability. People with disabilities have value. They matter. God loves them. They have souls. They need salvation. If this philosophy doesn't motivate our service, we'll be operating from the standpoint of service because parents ask us to do it, we feel sorry for the kids, or we want to increase overall attendance.

Psalm 139:13 doesn't have a footnote: "For you created my inmost being; you knit me together in my mother's womb." People with Fragile X syndrome, Down syndrome, and autism are all a part of God's creativity.

Mark 16:15 doesn't have a footnote either: "He said to them, 'Go into all the world and preach the good news to all creation.' " People with Fragile X syndrome, Down syndrome, and autism are a part of the church's responsibility to share the message to everyone regardless of ability.

> People with Fragile X syndrome, Down syndrome, and autism are all a part of God's creativity.

A children's minister asked me to visit his church to observe a child with serious emotional problems. When I arrived in the children's department on Sunday morning, I didn't have to be told where to go. I followed the screaming.

As I entered the classroom for second graders, the teacher with her back to the door was holding a screaming, kicking child. The other children were sitting quietly at the table. The teacher said, "You're hurting me, but I'm going to hold you until you calm down. Then I'll put you in your chair, and I'll tell you how much Jesus loves you."

I didn't need to tell that teacher how to handle the situation; she was doing it perfectly. She'd told the other students to be calm while she took care of the situation. And she took care of it beautifully.

That teacher understood the boy's problems and valued him as a human being. She worked to provide the care and education he needed. Today he's a wonderful family man, productive citizen, and faithful member of his church.

Share your plan to involve the leadership of your church.

Your church leadership needs to enthusiastically embrace the disability ministry. It's more than buying into a concept; it's buying into Jesus' attitude toward kids: "Let the little children come to me, and do not hinder them, for the kingdom of God belongs to such as these" (Mark 10:14).

Children with disabilities need to have their spiritual needs met. Disabilities shouldn't be a hindrance to involvement in the family of faith. Your leadership needs to see every child in its care as a valuable person who's loved by God.

It really isn't an option for a church to *not* have a disability ministry.

I'm saddened when parents tell me a church asked them not to return because of problems the staff encountered with their disabled child. Dr.

Jack Ballard, a minister with fifty-five years of experience and a friend of people with disabilities, offered a valuable insight when I asked him why churches don't universally include families experiencing disabilities. "I often wonder what response we might give if the Lord were to ask us why we didn't minister to him when he was disabled," Dr. Ballard said. "We might ask, 'When did we see you disabled?' Perhaps the Lord would answer, 'Each time you saw one of my disabled children!' "

Your pastor's positive involvement will be a key factor to the success of a special needs program. I've noticed that the strongest disability ministries are in congregations where the pastor considers it a vital part of the church's overall ministry plan.

One of the newest but fastest growing and most influential disabilities ministries I know is in a church whose pastor has a child with a severe disability. Similarly, one of the oldest ministries that I know was started in a church where the pastor, though not a parent of a child with a disability, adheres to the concept that every person is important and needs the love of God's people.

> Your pastor's positive involvement will be a key factor to the success of a special needs program.

And I know a pastor who didn't see the value of such a program early in his ministry. But when he became the grandfather of a child with a disabling condition, he became a champion of the cause.

When pastors see the value and become actively involved in a disability ministry, it tends to flourish. Get your church leadership on your team.

In a perfect world, this would happen routinely: During a volunteer training session in a large church's disability ministry, I was impressed to see that the deacon who oversaw the ministry was in attendance. He told us his role at the training was twofold: to pray for God's blessings on our activities and to stress the importance that church leadership placed on the ministry to families with special needs children.

Share how you'll find the people with disabilities in your congregation.

Don't be concerned about meeting the needs of every person with a disability in your community. Disability happens to people one person at a time.

Some of those people are in your church already—you just don't know it.

I was once asked to help a congregation start a program for three children who'd been identified as having disabilities. We took time to survey the church and discovered there were seventeen *other* children who fit our profile.

Here's a rule of thumb: between 10 and 15 percent of the population has a disability. That means if you have one hundred kids in your children's ministry, between ten and fifteen need attention. Find out who they are. And all it takes is a simple survey.

On your survey ask for a diagnosis, the child's age, contact information, and the child's present level of participation in your church.

Here's a rule of thumb: between 10 and 15 percent of the population has a disability.

Place the survey in your church paper or the bulletin. If you find a child with autism, another with cerebral palsy, and still another with a learning disability, start your planning with those children in mind. Begin with the people God has already brought you.

It's helpful to know the general trends in disabilities. They change. I can remember when children with speech problems were the leading recipients of special education services in schools. Today it's learning disabilities. Plus, there are more children with autism, behavior disorders, and health problems. Children are often diagnosed with ADD and ADHD (attention-deficit disorder with hyperactivity). Bipolar and oppositional defiant disorders appear frequently. Asthma and other allergy-related disorders are common and require the attention of the children's leaders.

Get to know the agencies in your community serving the disability population. Meet the families and the people they serve. Ask the agencies about their volunteer programs. Perhaps someone in the congregation works in a facility and could provide access. Let these agencies and their leaders know that your congregation welcomes the people they serve.

But begin first with the people God has already brought you.

Define and communicate your ministry model.

Develop a plan—not a program.

Start with this simple question: What will we do next Sunday morning if a couple arrives with two children: a nine-year-old boy with a disability and his eleven-year-old sister?

You already have a plan in place for the girl. You'll escort her to her age-appropriate Sunday school class. But what's your plan for her little brother?

You need a plan in place for children with disabilities that's as routine as your plan for children without disabilities. Here are some ideas:

- Include children with disabilities in regular classes using a buddy, an aide, or another one-on-one person.
- Develop a classroom that's designed for children until they become accustomed to the church routine and schedule.

- For the child with a disability who appears on Sunday unannounced, have people trained to assist him or her until a plan *can* be arranged.
- For cases in which children with severe disabilities or behavior problems attend your church, have a plan for working with them in a segregated group until they can handle placement in a regular classroom, or provide an in-home program.

Your plan is a beginning point. It's part of your ministry model—the philosophy that drives your overall approach to a disabilities ministry. As your overall model, I suggest inclusion. The term *inclusion* simply means making a place for children according to their ability to be part of their peer group.

Back in the 1960s, the school system provided special classes for specific disabilities. Teachers were trained to work with students with physical disabilities, emotional problems, or mental retardation. Teachers were all specialists in one area of disability.

Today teachers are more often trained to deal with a variety of disabilities. Including a child with a disability in a class with peers is the standard approach. As you talk with your church leaders about how creating a special needs ministry might impact your church, you'll probably hear three questions about creating a segregated program.

If you're a proponent of inclusion, you can give the following answers to these questions:

"How much will it cost?"

The cost of providing inclusive Christian education is the same as providing it for children who don't have disabilities. If a child's disability involves expensive medical equipment, the church won't have to provide it. Children's families will bring the equipment.

A wheelchair, a language board, a walker—devices the child uses every day—will be available on Sunday. If there's any additional cost, it will probably be in the form of a ramp, a wider door, or another accessibility modification. These are probably already a part of your local building code. If your building is up to ADA code, you're already in great shape.

If your building is up to ADA code, you're already in great shape.

The concern about expense stems from the days of providing Christian education in a separate classroom.

"Where do we get materials?"

Christian educators want materials to help them teach the message of Jesus' love, and your church probably provides it. And no matter what curriculum you buy, most teachers adapt it to fit their unique kids.

That's the same principle that applies for children with disabilities. Even if you buy curriculum that's been developed for children with disabilities, you'll need to adapt it to fit your unique kids.

So use the materials you're using now. As you include children with disabilities in classes with their age mates, consider making the following adaptations:

- For the student who's blind, put a part of the lesson into Braille.
- For the student who's visually impaired, enlarge the lesson on a copy machine or give the student a magnifying glass.
- For the student with a learning disability, color-code the parts of the lesson to be stressed. Use a highlighter or a transparency designed with colors to stress the main points of the lesson.
- For the students who have mental retardation, provide the materials even though they won't understand them. Don't give them materials that are beneath their age levels. Ask them to do the motor activities. Simplify a couple of activities, and have an assistant help them in completing them.

"Where do we find the extra space?"

You probably won't *need* any extra space if you're including children with disabilities in classes that already exist.

But depending on which children with disabilities God brings into your church, you might require a room. If so, whatever space you use for children without disabilities will probably work well. Make sure it's clean, bright, well-ventilated, and near a restroom. It also helps if the space is easily accessible, roomy, and noise free.

Address how you'll provide staff training.

Don't start your ministry without a staff training plan! Offer good information to teachers and assistants who'll work with children. You'll help them feel comfortable in their roles and have fewer surprises.

A rule of thumb: Train teachers in what they need to know for the specific child they'll be teaching or assisting. Include the following items:

- an overview of the disability
- the diagnosis of the child they'll be teaching
- information about allergies, communication level, likes and dislikes, what prompts misbehavior, and other information provided by the family
- some basic disability etiquette (p. 62)
- basic behavior-control techniques
- helpful teaching techniques
- ways to make the classroom a welcoming place
- information about the child's family
- a written job description, including how long the teaching assignment will last

And remind staff that they'll learn a *lot* from on-the-job training! *From the beginning, plan to treat your volunteers right. Here's how:*

- Provide adequate supervision.
- Meet as a group to evaluate, plan, and answer questions.
- Provide ongoing training.
- Reimburse expenses.
- Express appreciation—often.

Describe your plan for controlling behavior—in advance.

What will you do about disruptive behavior? Preventive planning makes it easier. Initially the plan is a written general behavior plan; it's then adapted for each child. Let your church leadership know that you'll be developing the general document, then adapting it for the children in your care. Your existing behavior plan will probably be adequate as a starting point.

Here are some steps that will give you valuable information as you adapt the general plan for children:

- Talk openly to parents and record the results. Ask about the nature of challenging behavior. Does the child hit, bite, throw objects, or run?
- Is the child on medication for the behavior?
- Does the child receive professional help? If so, ask for a copy of the behavior modification plan.
- What do the parents do to control challenging behavior?
- Train an adult to be with the child until the behavior is under better control.

Launching a Children's Special Needs Ministry

- If the child is on medication, ask the parents if he or she takes it on weekends. If the answer is no, ask for it to be administered then as well.

Describe how you'll communicate with families who have children experiencing disabilities—and families who don't.

Communicating with families is an essential ingredient to the success of your program. Be honest and direct. Tell the parents of children who have disabilities that you're not an expert in dealing with their children, but you want to learn. Explain that the church is interested in sharing the love of Jesus with the child. Ask for parents' help. Create an atmosphere of caring.

Avoid being judgmental and giving unsolicited advice. Use appreciative, accepting language. If you were a parent of a special needs child, would you rather hear, "What do you think God is punishing you for?" or "God knew what he was doing when he selected a strong person like you to have a special needs child."

Keep in mind you'll also have to communicate with families whose children *aren't* experiencing disabilities.

When the parents of a typical child hear that children with special needs are included in your classrooms, they may be concerned about the amount of attention their child will receive. They may wonder if their child will be hurt or mimic the behaviors of the child with a disability.

Reassure parents of typical children by telling them about the buddy system. Share that the teacher has an assistant. Encourage concerned parents to befriend the parents of the children with disabilities who are being included. They can also become advocates for the parents and their children with special needs and the church's inclusion of them.

Identify places for church members with disabilities to serve in your congregation.

Persons with disabilities who embrace faith and become a part of your church need to have a meaningful ministry. They become our brothers and sisters. Disability ministry is "ministry *with*" not "ministry *to*." A part of your role when you work with children is to provide avenues of service for all children, including children who have disabilities.

If you have an involved pastor, let that person know what sort of jobs persons with disabilities can do, and arrange a training program for those jobs.

An assignment in the church office, making favors for trays in a nursing home, passing out materials on Sunday morning, and similar jobs will make a person with disabilities feel a part of the church family.

An energetic children's minister shared a great idea with me. She arranged with ushers to train some of the children with disabilities to assist them on Sunday morning. Some of the children were able to do it on their own after a while. And the regular ushers learned a lot from their trainees.

Share your plan for transitioning students through the teen and adult departments of your church.

As you launch your disability ministry, keep in mind that children you serve will become teenagers and, in time, adults. Be sure senior staff members of the various age-group departments in your church's education program are ready to transition students with disabilities into their departments.

The truth is that children and adults often get positive attention and placement in most churches. However, social problems can arise when teenagers are called on to accept their peers with disabilities. There must be a plan to make smooth transitions.

> Keep in mind that children you serve will become teenagers and, in time, adults.

Include youth pastors in your planning committee. Make teenagers in your congregation aware of the needs of their peers who have disabilities. Ask the person in charge of adult education to be a part of the planning committee too.

I was asked by a children's pastor: "What do I do to get the youth department at my church interested in accepting students with disabilities who have come through the children's department?"

"That's a tough one," I responded.

I didn't know *how* tough. Before I could continue, she started to cry. Her statement was painful: "We have nurtured a boy with Down syndrome in the children's department since he was a baby. He's ready to go to the youth department. I stopped by the youth minister's office last week to talk about promoting him. I was stunned by the youth pastor's response. He said he didn't want the boy in his department and other arrangements would have to be made."

One solution for such an attitude is for the leadership of that church to articulate that regardless of disability, *everyone* is welcome. Then select staff who fit that philosophy.

Describe the rewards your church will experience because you have a disability ministry.

Children with disabilities can become Christians, though students with mental retardation have the most difficulty with religious concepts. Of this

Disability Etiquette
by Jim Pierson

How do I talk about disabilities?

Use the word *disability* rather than *handicap*. The word *handicap* has its origins in the sixteenth century when persons with disabilities were forced to beg for their livelihood. They stood on street corners with their caps in their hands. It's not a complimentary term.

Avoid the words *cripple*, *slow*, *crazy*, or other insensitive, archaic descriptions of disabilities. Expressions like "afflicted with" or "suffers from" lead to pity and sympathy, not respect and acceptance.

Use people-first language. Don't say "the disabled" or "the retarded." Rather say, "Jack has cerebral palsy" or "Anne has a vision problem."

When describing people who don't have a disability, stay away from the word *normal*. The terms "typical" or "a person without a disability" are more accurate and kinder.

And please: Don't describe people with disabilities as overly courageous, exceptionally brave, or superhuman.

How do I talk to a person with a disability?

Don't assume that a person with a disability

(continued)

group, 85 percent can be taught the facts about faith on a twelve-year-old level. And being part of a Christian education setting helps ensure a child's understanding of the elements of faith.

In cases in which the children's level of function is so low that they simply cannot comprehend basic facts, God understands. As in all situations, each person is surrounded by God's love and mercy. But in situations where the mental age is sufficient for learning, children should be taught in order to bring them to faith in Jesus.

A favorite memory of mine will always be Helen's baptism. Helen was part of a Sunday school program in a Christian college. The teacher assigned to Helen was a wonder. She drew pictures to illustrate the major parts of our Lord's life and ministry. The gospel lessons found a place in Helen's heart, which had not been affected by the cerebral palsy she had had from birth. After a few lessons, Helen told her teacher she wanted to become a Christian.

Wanting to be sure Helen understood the concept of baptism, the teacher requested that I talk with her. I asked her why she wanted to be baptized. In labored speech, Helen responded, "Be like Jesus."

She became one of the most vibrant Christians I've ever known. She enriched the lives of people around her. Her life was not one of disability but one of ability. She wasn't a victim of cerebral palsy; she was a victorious human being. Her life was evidence that her soul had been reconciled by the salvation made possible by Jesus, God's Son.

Helen died unexpectedly of pneumonia. A few days after her burial, her mother gave me the set of pictures the teacher had drawn to explain God's plan of reconciling the soul. As I looked through the pictures and lesson plans, I rejoiced that the goal had been met. Helen's wheelchair and communication devices were no longer needed. Her soul, freed from her flawed body, had returned to its Creator.

Just for You

Wouldn't it be great if everyone in the world saw things the same way we do? That because *we* see a critical need for a special needs ministry, *everyone else* sees it too?

Life's not always like that. It can be difficult to patiently explain the need, moving forward in baby steps instead of huge leaps and bounds.

- You want to meet *now*—the board schedules you on next month's agenda.
- You can picture a ministry reaching hundreds—the room you have can accommodate six.
- You see nothing but potential—the CE committee sees a long list of potential problems.

As you meet with leaders and talk with volunteers, you're making progress—even if it doesn't always feel that way. You're demonstrating by example that a special needs ministry is necessary. As you interact with a gentle persistence, you're demonstrating that the ministry is in good hands.

Be patient. Allow God time to work in other hearts, too.

(continued from page 62)
other than a hearing loss can't hear. We often respond to disabilities by speaking louder.

Don't assume that someone with speech, hearing, or physical problems has cognitive problems as well. Don't treat people with disabilities as if they're less intelligent than you are.

If you don't understand what someone is saying, just ask the person to repeat what was said. Use a friendly, "Would you run that past me again?" to make your point. If you absolutely can't understand, use a pencil and paper.

Talk directly with the person, not through a companion or a family member. As you learn your friend's world, the communication problems will diminish and comprehension will become easier.

Dear God,

Thank you for a vision and passion for special needs ministry. Please kindle that same vision and passion in others' hearts.

In Jesus' name, amen.

6. Getting the Word Out About Your Special Needs Ministry

by Pat Verbal

When it comes to communicating about your special needs ministry, you've really got three target audiences. You'll need to craft messages to each group; one message does *not* fit all.

Your three target audiences are

1. your church leadership,
2. your church membership, and
3. your community.

In Chapter 5 Jim Pierson discussed crafting a message to your church leadership. He identifies issues it cares about and suggests proactive ways to provide the information they need.

Don't fail to communicate clearly and often with your church leadership. As you keep them briefed, you'll provide the information and language they'll use to tell others what you're doing and why. They'll know what to say to families they meet who can benefit from your ministry. They're vitally important for many reasons, including...

You want leaders' blessings and prayers. Both spiritually and in terms of a budget, you want senior leadership in your church to embrace your ministry enthusiastically.

Leaders can open doors. You want a room for a class, and every square inch of the church building is already taken. But one word from your leadership and suddenly things get rearranged. You want their influence working for you, not against you.

As your leaders go, so goes your congregation. What leadership values tends to become what's preached from the pulpit, highlighted during announcements, and endorsed and encouraged in board meetings. Help your leadership discover the importance of your ministry, and they'll help you spread the word to the church membership and your community at large.

Involving your leadership can bring about dramatic results!

Pastor Brian Funk of Manor Brethren in Christ Church in Lancaster, Pennsylvania, agrees that a special needs ministry impacted him personally—and professionally.

"The summer of 2000 changed my life and ministry," says Pastor Funk. "I was invited to serve as pastor of the week at Spruce Lake Family Retreat." The retreat is for families with special needs children, a group Pastor Funk hadn't specifically served before.

Pastor Funk says, "My children, Chadd and Emily, were apprehensive about being there, but my wife, Roanne, and I were blown away. I had no idea what families with special needs children go through. The Lord touched our hearts, and we returned to our church knowing we had to do something to help."

> "I had no idea what families with special needs children go through."

After some preliminary groundwork, Pastor Funk formed a task force to determine what steps the church should take to become a disability friendly congregation. To introduce the new ministry to his church, he invited Doug Mazza, executive vice president of Joni and Friends, to speak during an awareness Sunday. Much of the planning was done by people affected by disabilities. Eventually the church's deacon board included a quadriplegic man and his wife.

Two years later, the church sent a team of twenty young people to work at the camp. "They've 'adopted' families from the retreat and maintained contact," says Pastor Funk. "A group of ten recently traveled to Maryland to give a surprise birthday party for a boy with cerebral palsy."

Not every pastor bonds so thoroughly with special needs ministry. But it does happen, and great things can come because of it.

Pastor Chris Spoor of Living Springs Community Church in Glenwood, Illinois, is a great example. The church's special needs ministry was launched as the congregation was designing a new facility.

"It was great," says Lori Swartwout, Friendship Ministry director at Living Springs and the mother of a twelve-year-old who has Down syndrome. "We were able to include everything we needed in the new building to meet ADA requirements. We have an elevator, handicap restrooms, wide halls, and even a ramp onto one side of the platform."

The church's special needs ministry was launched as the congregation was designing a new facility.

They started by establishing a special needs team, and then asked the congregation to complete a survey identifying the needs in the church and community. They also asked for volunteers willing to attend training classes. (See pages 77–78 for a sample of this brief survey.)

To Lori's amazement twenty-three people immediately volunteered. "God went before us," says Lori. "When that happens, it's sure to succeed. And Pastor Spoor supported us every step of the way."

Chris Spoor includes Lori in weekly staff meetings because he wants to see every decision through the eyes of the disabled. "We have a coffee house before and after services," says Pastor Spoor. "The table was located in the back of the room. Lori pointed out the narrow passages to the table were difficult for those in wheelchairs, so we immediately moved the table to the front of the room."

When the church scheduled a Disability Awareness Sunday, Pastor Spoor attended the planning sessions. A creative committee member suggested Pastor Spoor might preach from a wheelchair.

"I was happy to do it," says Pastor Spoor, "and I learned a valuable lesson. I got into a wheelchair as soon as I arrived at the church that day. During the first service, I pushed myself onto the platform. But in the second service, a member of our Friendship Ministry team pushed the chair for me. I found that a little more difficult to accept. To be passively dependent on someone else was a very humbling experience."

Think about the message this senior pastor illustrated for his congregation. It's no wonder the church doubled in attendance in just three years.

But Pastor Spoor is quick to point out, "We don't have a special needs ministry to grow numbers. We do it because it's the biblical mandate of the church of Jesus Christ. One of our core values is 'intentional inclusion' in every area. Some people think that just refers to race, but it also means abilities."

I asked Pastor Spoor what he would say to pastors who have concerns about starting a special needs ministry.

"Make up your mind to do it, and families will come," he said. "Don't do it, and they won't come! Some churches might be uptight about a physically disabled person greeting at the door on Sunday morning. Our church considers it a blessing."

Four sermon outlines for pastors (p. 143) and ten reproducible bulletin inserts (p. 154) are included in this book. Use the opportunity to give your pastor these tools as a chance to discuss your special needs ministry. Either your need for one, or your vision for the ministry that already exists.

Want to make an even bigger impression? Share the vision statement and goals that Friendship Ministries, a special needs ministry in Grand Rapids, Michigan, has crafted—and implemented. Ask your pastor which portions of the statement he or she agrees with and which seem suspect. If you're in agreement with what's printed to the right, it's very difficult to justify not actively seeking to support a special needs ministry.

Communicating With Your Church Membership

When it comes to making your congregation aware of the need for a special needs ministry, it's easy to hit the wrong target.

You *aren't* trying to just provide information about disabilities. Rather, your goal is to move people past fear and soften their hearts. Facts and figures about disability play a part in that process, but not the biggest part.

It's a transformation that only God can truly bring about. And it's very possible that no matter how focused your efforts, God ultimately uses someone other than you to help it happen.

How God Used a Four-Foot Spokesperson

Seven-year-old Taylor Garrison of Cornwall-on-Hudson, New York, became a spokesperson for children with special needs. When her sister,

---

Friendship's Vision

We believe everyone is created in God's image and can relate to God. We also believe salvation is a gift that is not dependent on a certain level of intelligence.

Our goals

- Students will experience the joy of knowing they are of value to God and to God's people.

- Students will grow in their understanding of God's world and their place in it.

- Students will grow in their relationship to Jesus Christ, claiming him as their Savior and Lord.

- Students will grow in their relationship with Christ's church, making a public profession of their faith and participating in the church's life and work.

Used by permission of Friendship Ministries, Grand Rapids, Michigan. www.friendship.org

Sierra, was born with Down syndrome, Taylor eagerly accompanied her parents to doctor visits and seminars. She soon discovered that some people avoided children with disabilities and that other children often teased them.

According to an article in Woman's World, Taylor didn't appreciate the situation. " 'You know how there are ten commandments?' Taylor says. 'Well, if I could make an eleventh, it'd be that we should help everyone in the world who's sick or different.' "

Taylor gives informative presentations at schools about Down syndrome. She's making a difference in her sister's world by helping dispel myths about children with special needs.

An even more unusual "spokesperson" is Whiskers, a wirehair terrier whose hind legs were paralyzed when she got hit by a car. A couple at the Cornerstone Free Methodist Church in Akron, Ohio, gave Whiskers her life back by making a cart for her hind legs. Whiskers is now a mascot for the church's "Count Me In" special needs ministry.

> "We believe that God sees abilities and gives each of us a spirit not limited in its capacity to receive or give God's love."

"We call our ministry 'Count Me In' for people who are often counted out by society," says director Carol Tolson. Carol herself is physically challenged and has been an advocate for disabilities since 1976.

"People always say our church is so friendly. I think that's because our hope at Cornerstone is that everyone can find 'The Father, a Family, and a Fulfilling Future.' We believe that God sees abilities and gives each of us a spirit not limited in its capacity to receive or give God's love."

Churches with friends like Taylor, Carol, and Whiskers are fortunate because their personalities shine and draw attention to the special needs ministries. Do you have someone in your church who would make an equally effective ambassador? If so, are you giving that person an opportunity to serve?

How Aware Is Your Church Membership of Special Needs Children?

Terese M. Abrams, whose daughter has Down syndrome, suggests that institutions such as churches aren't always aware that they've failed to lay out a welcome mat for children with disabilities. The lack of warmth isn't intentional; the church simply doesn't understand.

Ms. Abrams suggests that churches and institutions fall into one of five categories, based on their level of inclusion.

Into what category would you place your church?

Level One: Institutional Unawareness

This church feels exempt from any need to open its programs to children with special needs, if it feels anything at all. The issue of what to do for special needs children and their families hasn't come up.

Were parents to bring a child with special needs to ask an usher what Sunday school class the child should attend, they'd receive a puzzled look. And they might hear, "We don't have anything for those sort of children."

In this case, ignorance is definitely *not* bliss—at least for families with special needs children.

Level Two: Institutional Tolerance

Children with special needs are allowed to attend events at this church, but the leadership probably has no idea how to adapt activities and classes so children with disabilities can participate. Special needs children are nearly always cast in the role of observers.

Level Three: Inter-Institutional Separation

Children with special needs are welcome but assigned token roles. And while children might enjoy activities and classes, they aren't really included into the programs.

In many settings, the special needs children are segregated from the typical children, even when integration would be easily achievable. The church may try to create a "separate but equal" setting, believing that a little six-year-old with Down syndrome has more in common with a twelve-year-old child with ADHD than with children her own age.

Level Four: Institutional Support

Church leaders seek ways to involve children with special needs and accept them into the group. There's integration of special needs children into classrooms with typical children whenever possible. But either because of a lack of training or prejudice, classroom leaders' expectations are still too low.

Level Five: Interdependent Groups

Children with special needs are full members in the life of this church. They sing on the worship team for children's church. They go on field trips and serve as teacher helpers. They see adults with disabilities serving in leadership positions and want to be like them.

Do a candid self-assessment of your church, and then ask families in your church who have children with special needs to tell you how you're doing. How do your scores compare? What does that tell you?

For your church to grow in acceptance of children with special needs, you've got to overcome some barriers. Here are some suggestions:

If you're a level one, an institutionally unaware church...

The first obstacle you need to overcome if you want your church to be a welcoming place that includes children with special needs is to raise awareness of the need.

Ask your pastor to make use of the ten photocopiable bulletin inserts provided in chapter 14. Suggest that the issue of including people with special needs be raised from the pulpit, too—perhaps using the sermon outlines included in chapter 13. Few pastors want to be told what to present from the pulpit, however. Be sure your suggestion is a request, not a demand.

Consider organizing a Disability Ministry Sunday, including a worship service that heightens the awareness of disability. Invite people to share testimonies about how God's grace helped them overcome troubles. Plan Sunday school lessons that focus on Jesus' attitude and ministry to people with disabilities. Invite disabled children and adults to sing, read Scripture, and pray. But if your church hasn't let people with disabilities serve publicly in the past, it may be uncomfortable for everyone involved unless you raise awareness throughout the year through sermons and service opportunities. Let the Disability Ministry Sunday be the *culmination* of your efforts, not the only thing you do.

> Plan Sunday school lessons that focus on Jesus' attitude and ministry to people with disabilities.

If no people with special needs are in your church, you might arrange to screen one of the films listed at the end of this chapter. Or you might begin by inviting children, youth, or adults from an area group home to attend this special worship service. Treat them as honored guests, and include them in the worship service.

Your goal is to help your congregation see that people with special needs exist. You want to break through indifference, denial, or fear. People fear what they don't understand, and that includes disabilities. Fear may be expressed as cold distancing, active avoidance, or extreme self-centeredness. All the comments below include an element of fear.

- "My daughter won't learn as much in Sunday school if she's with children who are *obviously* below her level."

- "We're not qualified to care for babies who have feeding tubes."
- "Families with special needs children will be a drain on our congregation."
- "People who use sign language in worship are a distraction to others."
- "That church across town is better suited to serve *those* children."
- "Teachers won't volunteer to serve in classes with special needs children."

Gently work to remove the fear or prejudice that often is behind these comments.

These sorts of comments might appear cruel or indifferent, but remember: The people making the comments are brothers and sisters in Christ. They're members of the church. God is working in their lives as certainly as he's working in yours. Don't react with anger or deliver a lecture. Rather, gently work to remove the fear or prejudice that often is behind these comments.

Bulldozing over people to put a program in place isn't the best option. Those people will simply be silenced; they won't become supporters. They won't provide the welcoming smiles you want children with special needs to experience in your church.

If you're a level two, an institutionally tolerant church...

Your teachers and other leaders need an education, and nobody can provide that faster than children who have special needs.

Consider what happened at a church in Allen, Texas, when three-year-old Wakeland Stickens showed up.

This little fellow is developmentally delayed, but he's fast—not because his legs are strong, but because they're weak. Wakeland compensates for his weak legs with a four-wheel walker. When he rolls through the church foyer, adults step aside with a smile. Other children run along beside him trying to say, "Hi."

One Wednesday night his mom, Joanna, found Wakeland's walker standing alone in the church gym. When she located her son, she found he'd traded his walker for a pair of tennis shoes equipped with built-in wheels. Wakeland had one shoe on each hand and was fearlessly venturing into a spirited game of basketball.

"The people at our church have been very accepting," says Joanna. "The initial adjustment was very hard for my husband and me. Our pastors pray for us and work to mainstream Wakeland into all the children's ministry programs. He's a very determined little boy who loves to sing 'Jesus Loves Me' and 'Deep and Wide.' "

The Stickens family has taken an active role in the church, and that's opened the eyes—and hearts—of fellow church members. The Stickens' lives send a valuable message: "We're OK. We accept God's sovereignty and if we can do it, you can too."

Children in the church are more likely to accept life's challenges without blaming God because they've *seen* the Stickens do it. They've *experienced* the enthusiasm and joy of Wakeland. What a shame to think Wakeland might not be welcomed in some churches.

> Don't get frustrated if some members of your church don't warm up to special needs children right away.

But here's a caution you need to take to heart: *It takes time.* Don't get frustrated if some members of your church don't warm up to special needs children right away. It can be awkward for typical families to suddenly come face to face with a child in a wheelchair. What do they say? What if they say the wrong thing?

You can provide the transitions people need. Take people aside who you've seen struggle, and say, "I saw you talking with Dylan, and you looked a bit nervous. May I share a few insights with you that will help you feel more comfortable next time? I appreciate your reaching out to him, and I want to encourage you to continue doing it."

You can provide the ideas that teachers may not have about including special needs children. Be positive, upbeat, and encouraging. Help teachers get the skills they need.

Build some adaptive opportunities into your church programming. Offer a course in ASL in the youth department. Teenagers who take it (even if they take it for the wrong reason—to be able to talk to friends without their parents or teachers knowing what they're saying!) can become volunteers in the children's area.

Train ushers and greeters at your church to use proper disability etiquette. See that they ask before offering assistance and never patronize. Help them to develop habits that keep them from startling children by coming up to them from behind or talking too close to their faces. Train them to identify themselves first and to be specific and clear when giving directions. And most of all, to relax and enjoy the special needs children they meet.

If you're a level three, an inter-institutional separation church...

The chief challenge you'll face is helping your leaders move past segregation to inclusion when it's possible. It's a philosophical difference and can be a challenge to change.

When you segregate children, you reinforce their feelings...

- that they're somehow unacceptable to typical children; that they're broken or incomplete.
- that they can't have relationships with typical children.
- that they're worthy only of being cared for; they have nothing to offer to typical children.

Are these the messages this church wanted to send? Absolutely not! The church probably adopted a segregation model because it made life easier for the teaching staff to have all the more challenging kids in one room. The church thought it was helping the children, too, by having a more highly trained teaching staff available to them.

If this church moves to an inclusion model, there *will* be more challenges in more rooms—so there needs to be more training. There may be a need for more volunteers as you put "buddies" with the special needs children who can use them. And you still may have to maintain a separate room for children who have medical issues that require them to be closely monitored.

Or you can consider this: Visit the children with severe disabilities at home. Send trained teachers to make home visits that will brighten up the child's day and assist parents in providing Christian education to their children. While this isn't necessarily a best-case alternative, it's one to keep in mind. Offer it to parents; perhaps it will best meet their needs. And what a ministry for a master teacher who wants to make a significant difference in a child's life!

Also find nonthreatening ways to bring families of special needs children and typical children together. Hold an inclusive VBS, ice-cream party, and field trip. Tell anyone who's worried about inclusion that these activities are experiments or pilot programs. By using these terms, you communicate that it's not a permanent situation—you're monitoring the events to see how things go.

> Find nonthreatening ways to bring families of special needs children and typical children together.

Be intentional about having children interact at the events. Encourage friendships to develop and for children and families to see how much they have in common. When the time comes to suggest inclusion replace segregation, you'll have several successes that demonstrate it can work!

One church encouraged people to sign up to help out with a party at a nursing home. Many nursing homes care for severely disabled young people as well as the elderly, and this provided a wonderful activity for the children with special needs and typical children to do together.

What can you do to have your kids—all your kids—hang out together?

If you're a level four, an institutionally supportive church...

You're nearly there. All that may be missing is training—learning how to go about turning a good program into a great one. And here's something to consider: You might not be the person to do the training!

Unless you're an educator who's trained to work with special needs children, there are probably things about how to include special needs children that you don't know. Even if you *are* a trained educator, it's possible there are things you don't know.

Bring in a top-notch resource person for training. The person may be from your local school system or a college instructor. It's not absolutely essential that the person even be a believer—you're asking that person to share information about special needs, not deliver a devotion. And the fact that your church is so committed to including special needs children may be a tremendous testimony to the resource person. Be sure to invite that person to see your program in action by coming back on a Sunday morning.

If you're a level five, an interdependent group church...

May God bless your ministry and multiply it a hundredfold. On behalf of all the lives you're touching, thank you.

Perhaps you've noticed that communicating with your congregation requires more than just announcements and bulletin inserts—though they're a good idea.

Softening a church's heart toward special needs children and welcoming them requires God's love accepted and then God's love expressed. That's work only God can do, but you can certainly assist by praying consistently and making yourself available to serve as needed.

As always, pray. Build a team. Keep listening to God to make sure you're building the ministry his way, in his timing, for his purposes.

Communicating With Your Community

How do you make people aware of the presence of a special needs ministry at your church? Where do you begin?

For starters, *don't* buy a television ad or put money into radio commercials unless your church already airs commercials that you can piggyback on to without cost. The people you're trying to reach may or may not see or hear your message that way—and it will cost you a fortune. And while stations often run public service announcements, those may air at two in the morning.

It *is* a good idea to let Christian radio stations know of your program; suggest that they might want to do a news story about it. You'll get much more airtime with no cost at all!

Be sure that every time the name of your church is presented to the general public—in the Yellow Pages, newspaper ads, fliers, bulletins, on letterhead, and on the church sign by the street—that the words *Special Needs Ministry* are present. Not everyone who reads the information will understand precisely what it means, but to people you're trying to reach, the words will shine out like a beacon.

The good news is that the people you want to meet are connected and networked. The best way to make them aware of what you offer is to notify those networks and make it easy for the networks to distribute information.

A one-page flier is an easy way to give the essential information and to invite informational phone calls. Be clear about your church being inclusive if that's the case.

A sample flier is on page 76. Adapt it as necessary, and provide copies to group homes and organizations in your community that address the needs of special needs children.

> Attend all walk-a-thons and fund-raisers for special needs in your community.

Each time an organization agrees to post or distribute the fliers, ask what other organizations might be appropriate to contact. Who else cares about providing positive experiences to special needs children? You may discover agencies, organizations, and networks that you've never heard of.

Attend all walk-a-thons and fund-raisers for special needs in your community. Having a booth and providing cups of cool water to participants on a 10K fund-raiser for Muscular Dystrophy, diabetes, or even to raise money for a group home, puts you in direct contact with people who care about children and adults with special needs. Become a presence in their lives.

Your Children Are Welcome!

We believe that all children are created in God's image. Every child has value to God—and us!

If you want your child to grow in an understanding of his or her value to God and to enjoy time with other children in an inclusive Sunday school setting, join us for Sunday school at First Christian Church.

You'll find...

- a warm, welcoming atmosphere;

- trained teachers who'll give your child caring, personal attention;

- a congregation that understands the challenges of caring for a special needs child; and

- an ongoing opportunity for your child to make friends.

Please call Tiffany at (555) 555-1234 for more information. And let us know about your child—we want to welcome your child by name!

The Sunday School Department
First Christian Church
123 Anytown Lane
Yourtown, Pennsylvania 12345

Permission to photocopy this flier from *Special Needs—Special Ministries* granted for local church use. Copyright © Group Publishing, Inc., P.O. Box 481, Loveland, CO 80539. www.grouppublishing.com

And by all means, give copies of the flier to any family you're already serving; they probably know other children and families who would be interested.

If you're unsure what your church membership knows about special needs, the following survey will be of help. Ask church members to complete the survey in the context of a church service. If you let people take the surveys home and ask that they be returned, you'll receive few completed surveys!

This is a general survey, so it may not meet all your needs. The first section explores personal awareness of special needs.

The second section will help you determine the perceived need for a special needs ministry in your church.

Sample Survey

Part 1:

____ I have a child with special needs in my family.

Please comment on the nature of the disability. _____

_____

_____

____ I know of children with disabilities in my neighborhood.

How many children? _____

What sort of disabilities do they have? _____

_____

_____

____ I do not personally come in contact with children with disabilities.

Part 2:

____ Our church is currently assisting families with disabled children.

____ Our church currently has disabled children active in our Sunday school program.

____ Our church doesn't have any children with disabilities.

____ I'd like to see our church do more in the area of a children's special needs ministry (working with children who have disabilities).

In what areas? _____

_____

Why are these areas of interest to you? _____

_____

(continued on page 78)

OK TO COPY

Sample Survey (continued)

Part 3:

_____ I have experience working with children who have special needs.

What sort of experience do you have? _____

_____

_____

_____

_____ I'd be willing to attend a training class to learn more about ministry to children with disabilities.

_____ I know of other churches in our area that have Christian education programs which involve children with special needs.

What churches? _____

_____ I'm willing to serve on a prayer and planning team that has as a goal developing a children's special needs ministry at our church.

Name _____ Date _____

Phone _____ E-mail _____

OK TO COPY

The third section explores the willingness of the survey respondent to become personally involved.

Because you can assume that not everyone will know what *special needs* means, the term *disabilities* is used as well, though it's not defined. How people complete this survey will help you determine how *disability* is understood by your congregation. That's helpful information if you define attention-deficit disorder as a disability, but your church doesn't.

Be sure you add questions that will help you find out what you really want to know. You probably won't be allowed to survey the church again. Make your first effort count—draft a survey that's been thought through and provides information you can use to make decisions for your church.

Just for You

Communication is a two-way street. You want to shout the news about your special needs ministry from the rooftops, and that's good. But you also need to keep listening throughout that process.

Listen to your church leadership. Listen to the families you're serving. Listen to the leading of the Lord.

Ultimately, it's the *listening* you do that will bear the most fruit. Why? Because you're talking to such diverse audiences. And because a special needs ministry is one of loving care—and nothing communicates that more than a genuine desire to listen.

God bless you as you listen and as you share the good news.

Recommended videos that will help you raise awareness in a non-threatening way:

Blessings Out of Brokenness, a four-part video series by Joni Tada (1-818-523-5777).

The Finger Food Cafe Show: A Grand Opening. This hour-long program is packed with great songs and Bible stories. It's presented in ADL, voice, and open English captions. Produced by Deaf Missions (712) 322-5493; www.DeafMissions.com.

Dear God,

We want to do so much — and we need so much help to make it happen. Thank you that you already know who you'll be calling into this special needs ministry. We ask you for patience, enthusiasm, and wisdom — all of which you have in abundance. And all of which you're willing to share with us.

In Jesus' name, amen.

7. Recruiting and Training Volunteers

by Pat Verbal

My passion for investing in children with special needs started in 1991. That's the year I became children's pastor at a church that had a special needs ministry.

Supervising a program of twenty-five children, ages two to fifteen, changed my life. My husband and I served as substitute teachers when the class' regular teachers were absent.

We quickly discovered the special needs children loved doing everything a regular class did, but they needed a little more help—as well as more hugs, laughter, puppets, music, and fun. The class, the Royal Hearts Club, met on Wednesday evenings while parents enjoyed a support group. We were active volunteers, but still had a certain distance from the children.

Two years later, a precious little girl with Down syndrome became part of our own family. Jessica won our hearts instantly, and the ministry at church took on an entirely new perspective. Then it became intensely personal. And it's stayed personal ever since.

For you to have a special needs program in your church, you need staff. And if your church is like most, those staff will be volunteers. I'd like to share with you some ideas for finding volunteers—the *right* volunteers—and then training them so they're effective in ministry.

Where Do You Find Volunteers for Special Needs Classes?

They may come from anywhere—but you need to make sure they're the right people and that you provide the right training.

Our Royal Hearts Club was started by two special education teachers who worked at a state-funded school. These trained professionals wanted their church family to welcome the special needs community, so they volunteered to create a place for special needs children at church. As the ministry grew, people who never dreamed of serving in a special needs ministry began to enjoy the great kids...and be drawn into the ministry.

Having trained teachers establish and staff your special needs ministry is one way to get started, but it's uncommon. We were blessed with a ready-made, already trained staff: Professionals passionate about volunteering their skills. If God also blesses you this way, be grateful!

If you've informed your congregation about the opportunities based on your survey results, then you may already have a short list of people interested in your special needs ministry. They're *interested*, but not *committed*. See if there are any special needs professionals in your stack, and involve them in the planning of your ministry right away. Even if they're unable to help staff your ministry, they can give you guidance about how to determine what you need, who you need, and how to proceed.

> Often it's the parents of special needs children who offer the most help.

Often it's the parents of special needs children who offer the most help. They want their children to have fulfilling experiences in church, and they're experts regarding their children's needs.

Plus, these parents can spot an adult who has an open heart for children with disabilities a mile away. They're drawn to people and programs that are kind to their children. Sometimes the friendships that form between those parents become the beginning of a church's special needs ministry.

And sometimes it's a special needs child who creates a culture in which *everyone* develops a tender heart for individuals with special needs. A ministry forms naturally.

One of my childhood friends had an older sister who had Down syndrome. In our small church everyone knew when Kathy walked in. She moved from pew to pew, hugging everyone in sight. Her mumbled greetings could be heard above everyone—and everything—else.

As teenagers we were embarrassed when visitors showed up. Yet, as we all learned to look out for Kathy, in many ways our whole church became a special needs ministry. Nobody recruited or trained us. We just did what came naturally, in response to having Kathy with us.

Years later, when I talk to someone from that church, Kathy's name always comes up. She made an impression on our lives because her family and our church loved her just as she was. And somehow, even as a child, I understood God loved her in that way too.

Your volunteers may come from the ranks of professionals who attend your church. They may be parents, church staff members, or people you'd never suspect value a special needs ministry.

But unless you're intentional about communicating with and recruiting volunteers, it's unlikely you'll get the right people on board. And unless you're intentional about training your volunteers, it's unlikely they'll do the right things once they're working with children.

It all starts with finding the right people, so answer this question: If God sent you the ideal volunteers for your church's special needs ministry, what would those people be like?

How to Find the Right Volunteers

Start with job descriptions.

Create job descriptions for each ministry opportunity you want to fill. Unless you're specific about who you need, how will you recognize the right person if he or she appears? It's important that you think through a number of issues:

- What time commitment is involved? How many hours per week?
- What's the duration of the commitment? a year? two years? a week?
- What's the child contact involved? Will this volunteer be a one-on-one buddy or the leader of a group that includes other volunteers who have primary child contact?
- Will the role be one of "pioneer," someone who's creating a new class or program? Or is the role one of assistant to a trained teacher? Those two roles require very different skills!

- Will the person specialize in one disability? two? Or serve in a classroom that includes a broad mix of needs?
- Will the role include home visits or leading support groups?
- To whom will the person report? What sort of evaluations can the person expect? What sort of training?

Creating a job description forces you to think through exactly what you're asking people to do. And, of course, it makes recruiting the right people easier because they can see if your expectations match their abilities and interests.

It'd be great if you could pluck a staff of trained professionals from your congregation—but the fact is you don't necessarily need professionals.

What you need are ordinary people who are willing to become everyday heroes in the lives of children.

My favorite TV neighbor, Mr. Rogers, went to be with the Lord after three decades of ministry to children. I think he said it best when, in an interview quoted in The Dallas Morning News, he said, "We live in a world in which we need to share responsibility. It's easy to say, 'It's not my child, not my community, not my world, not my problem.' Then there are those who see the need and respond. I consider those people my heroes."

Move Potential Volunteers Past Fear

One obstacle you'll need to overcome with potential volunteers is fear.

Many people are literally afraid of special needs children. Potential volunteers may be afraid a child will have a physical or emotional need the volunteer can't handle. Potential volunteers might think they have to be doctors or therapists to effectively lead in a special needs classroom.

Not true; but volunteers will never know unless you tell them.

Remove obstacles that might keep someone from volunteering.

So begin your recruiting by designing an ad for your church bulletin, newsletter, or Web site that describes the sort of people you'd like on your team and what skills they need. If you'll train people, say so. Remove obstacles that might keep someone from volunteering.

Your ad might read along these lines:

Join Our Special Needs Ministry Team!

We're looking for people who…

- love and accept children just as they are.
- are motivated, excited, and enthusiastic about being with and learning from these special children.
- desire one-on-one relationships with children who allow us to be part of their faith journeys.
- display high energy, creativity, and patience, and who believe special needs children can love God and serve their world.
- long to share God's own heart and learn how to bring hope and healing to families who feel "left out" at church.

We'll provide the training you need to be effective and comfortable in this ministry. *You* provide the love!

Look for Volunteers Who Have Servants' Hearts and Christ's Love

Some things you can train people to do, and some things you can't.

You can't work in or around a nursing home or hospital long before you sort out who went into medicine for the money and who was motivated by a desire to serve others.

Usually it's the bedpans that are the giveaway.

Nobody likes to empty bedpans. It's a nasty job under the best of circumstances, so how much someone enjoys this task isn't the point. *Nobody* enjoys the task.

It's *how* bedpans are emptied that can tell you volumes about the person doing the job. Some medical staff look offended and mutter to themselves the entire time they're dealing with the bedpan. And that leaves the patient feeling awful.

Other staff members take it all in stride and actually talk with the patients. They make sure patients don't feel guilt or shame about something over which they have no control. Their medical staff are servants— and *they're* doing ministry.

Look for volunteers who you think would consider bedpans as ministry. Training people what to *do* in your ministry isn't all that hard; it's a matter of building skills and experience. But you can't train a proper *attitude* for doing ministry. That sort of loving, caring heart takes a work of God.

Consider Using Volunteers Who Don't Attend Your Church

I'm not suggesting that you bring non-Christians on board to do Christian education, but *do* be open to using people who may not be a part of your congregation.

If the parent of a special needs child wants to help you and that parent belongs to another church, be open to using that parent. Your church may have a rule that only church members can teach, and there's wisdom in that stipulation. But in your situation, you may have staff who don't actually teach—they provide technical or medical coverage for severely handicapped children. They're already comfortable, dependable people in the lives of the children.

Might they be allowed to be present in the classroom?

How to Provide the Right Training

Once you've got the right people involved in your special needs ministry—people who love kids just the way God created them, who love God, and who are committed to serving families—you want to make sure they're effective.

That requires training. *Appropriate* training. Volunteers don't need to study until they have the equivalent of a degree in special education.

Training volunteers to serve children with special needs can be as simple as talking with parents and following their advice next Sunday. Or it can be a lifelong learning process that builds your skills—and the skills of your volunteers.

But know this: There's no one approach to working with special needs children. Each child is a unique individual who requires a unique ministry plan.

"We had one child who is profoundly autistic," says Pastor Rick Roberts of Trinity Church in Sunnyvale, California. "When he came to church, we had someone assigned each week specifically to minister to him. He was hurting the other children, so we weren't able to integrate him into the classroom. Another child in our program has autism, but other than being somewhat of a discipline challenge, he integrates fairly well."

Two children and two completely different strategies for serving those children. The fact is that each case of special needs is different and requires a separate evaluation to see how much the child can integrate into existing classes versus needing individual attention and care. That's why we're not offering a turnkey, ready-to-go training session in this book: There isn't any such session. There are definitely issues you need to address, and we bring those to your attention. But there's no one-size-fits-all training that will transform your leaders into fully prepared special ministries staff.

The training you provide depends on what children come to your program. It's an individual thing. But generally speaking, it's wise to provide training for five broad categories of disability. Start by making sure everyone has at least a working knowledge of these disability categories and how to respond to them:

1. Children with physical disabilities

Children with physical disabilities need to understand that they are more than just their bodies. That is, their bodies (like yours) are containers for their souls, where they *really* live.

A soul is everything we think and feel on the inside.

Physical disabilities include cerebral palsy, spina bifida, muscular dystrophy, dwarfism, brittle bone disease, injuries, and health disorders.

Children with physical disabilities generally like to participate in all classroom activities, so you'll need to provide training that helps your volunteers assist children by anticipating their struggles and planning alternative ways to play games or do crafts.

A soul is everything we think and feel on the inside.

Volunteers also need to be prepared to handle bladder and bowel functions. Don't assume a tour of duty in the nursery will prepare your staff for this; they're dealing with older children who have social needs surrounding this issue, as well as physical needs.

Autism spectrum disorders are developmental disabilities that you might want to address in training. ASDs are brain dysfunctions often characterized by delays in language and communication development and difficulty with social interactions. Functioning levels range from extremely severe to mild, and ASD is relatively common. The Centers for Disease Control and Prevention estimated that in 2002, one person among every 250 to 300 individuals born will have an autism spectrum disorder. ASD needs to be on your radar.

And with ASD or any other sort of special need, it's important to train volunteers to ask questions in a sensitive fashion and use proper terminology when discussing a student's disabilities.

2. Children with hearing impairments

Hearing loss can be mild, moderate, or severe. Some children with hearing loss retreat into their own worlds and may also struggle with language development. Memorizing Scriptures is one way to encourage speech and build a student's self-image.

Train volunteers to be sure they have a hearing-impaired child's attention before speaking. A good strategy is to step closer to the child rather than raising your voice. Train staff to also maintain good eye contact and use a normal voice without exaggerated mouth movements. And before volunteers interact with a child, it's important to know whether a child uses sign language. Parents will gladly tell you the best way to communicate with their children.

And set your volunteers up for success by using a classroom that has few background noise distractions.

3. Children with visual disabilities

Children who are visually impaired are often gifted with a heightened sense of awareness that helps them adapt to their surroundings. These children may use corrective glasses or lenses. In many ways they're emotionally the same as other students in your class, but they often require a little more time to grasp lessons.

Volunteers need training to learn how to adapt a lesson for nonvisual learners. Clearly, there's no benefit to hanging up a Bible timeline poster, but a teacher may still want children to know the information. How can that teacher communicate it?

One option is for you to provide large print or Braille Bibles. Some students may use magnifiers, so have them available. But keep in mind that to read Braille, one must memorize sixty-three configurations, so don't rush students.

Teach volunteers to turn visual lessons into hands-on experiences. Instruction can involve music, bells, or beepers rather than lights or other visual cues.

It may also be important that students have a classmate "buddy" to help when leaders are introducing new concepts or using videos.

4. Children with learning disabilities

Learning disabilities are often accompanied by emotional and behavioral problems. Disorders affect how children process what they see and hear. Learning disabilities you may encounter include ADD, ADHD, dyslexia, and academic skill disorders. These children try hard, but can't keep up with their peers because of problems with perception, memory, attention, and immaturity.

Learning disabilities are sometimes called hidden disabilities because children look fine.

Learning disabilities are sometimes called hidden disabilities because children look fine. The disabilities aren't obvious.

Volunteers need training that helps them see beyond the obvious. Children with learning disabilities aren't likely to sit still for long periods of time or keep track of their belongings. It's helpful if volunteers learn to create and maintain schedules children can trust and can become comfortable with. Surprises aren't always a good idea.

Volunteers must adapt activities to steer clear of paper and pencils and become adept at giving single-task instructions and using repetition. Encourage volunteers to always praise the children, no matter how small children's efforts may be.

5. Children with intellectual impairments

Children who are intellectually impaired represent various mental retardation and communication disorders such as Down syndrome, fetal alcohol syndrome, hydrocephaly, and Fragile X syndrome. These students have the ability to grow and learn and can make a positive impact on their world.

They can know who God is and who Jesus is. They can become familiar with the heroes of the Bible, understand Bible events, appreciate Christian music, and participate in prayer. They can each have a relationship with peers and with Jesus.

Your goal is to teach your volunteers to believe that intellectually challenged children can indeed learn.

How to Find Training for Your Volunteers

How can you possibly hold monthly or quarterly training sessions that meet the specific needs of each special needs teacher? You probably can't—but you *can* provide a variety of training options directly related to the special needs in your church. And you may not have to create the training sessions yourself.

Here are some training opportunities that can inform and bless your volunteers:

Visit community support groups.

Many groups meet monthly to discuss issues that affect the special needs community, and some groups are hosted by churches. Check the local newspaper for times and locations. Visit and see if perhaps you can arrange for the appropriate volunteers to participate or be trained through the group.

Here's a list of some of the organized support groups that might welcome church volunteers who want to be more informed and effective: Attention Deficit Disorder Association, Autism Society, Parents of Bipolar Children support groups, Better Breathing Club, National Diabetes Education Program, and the Allergy and Asthma Network.

Visit the special needs program in another church.

It's a sacrifice to have one volunteer miss your program for a month, but if another church is doing effective special needs ministry, it may be worthwhile to have a volunteer shadow teachers there. Especially if you're launching a program, this can shorten your volunteers' learning curves.

Invite guest speakers to lead training seminars at your church.

Doctors, nurses, parents, authors, and special education teachers all have expertise to share. And many charge a minimal fee or no fee at all. Tap your network of support groups, and ask leaders who they'd recommend.

Take advantage of Christian education conferences that provide a special track for special needs ministries.

If you can't afford to send everyone, be sure that whoever goes buys the relevant tapes and passes along what was learned through a training session for the rest of your volunteers.

A few tips: Make sure that the conference attendee understands that a professional summary following the conference is expected. That way relevant information can be collected and organized as the conference unfolds.

Also ask that the person collect business cards from people at the workshops who attend churches of similar size or who have challenges that resemble those you're facing. The business cards can be used to make contacts that will provide information—and inspiration!

And you'll want to have the training session within a few weeks of the conference. Even the best-prepared presenter will begin to forget details just a few days after returning from the conference.

Create a training library.

Include books such as *Creative Plan Activities for Children with Disabilities,* by Lisa Rappaport Morris and Linda Schultz (Human Kinetics Books) and Dr. Jim Pierson's book *Exceptional Teaching: A Comprehensive Guide for Including Students With Disabilities* (Standard Publishing).

Be sure volunteers know that these resources are available for their use, and encourage volunteers to use them.

Find and use resources in community training libraries.

Many metropolitan areas have children's hospitals that sponsor support groups for the parents of disabled children. Check with hospitals to see what training resources they provide. And if a child has a specific diagnosis, contact organizations that are advocates for that diagnosis. Many community organizations have books, videos, and handouts that can help your volunteers. These resources are often available for loan at no cost.

Hit the Internet, and find information to pass along.

Training manuals, seminars, and tapes are available through many denominational and independent groups. Here's a brief list to get you started.

- The Christian Reformed Church: Committee on Disability Concerns (www.crcna.org)
- Church of the Brethren (www.brethren.org/abc)
- Church of the Nazarene (www.nazarene.org)
- American Baptist Church, USA (www.abc-usa.org)
- Episcopal Disability Network (www.edn4ministry.org)
- Evangelical Lutheran Church (www.elca.org)
- Friendship Ministries (www.friendship.org)
- Joni and Friends Ministry (www.joniandfriends.org)
- Lutheran Special Education Ministries (www.comnet.org)
- Presbyterian Church (USA) (www.pcusa.org)
- Reformed Church in America (www.rca.org)
- Southern Baptist Convention (www.sbc.net)
- Special Touch Ministries (www.specialtouch.org)

A caution: Not every Web site includes accurate information. Be sure that you're surfing only sites that have reliable contributors and that are associated with credible organizations. Let the Web surfer beware!

Finding volunteers for a special needs ministry isn't just a numbers game. It's far better to have too few volunteers than to have the wrong volunteers.

You must find people who have a heart and passion for a special needs ministry. People who love God and will share God's love with children. People who will invest the time and effort it takes to connect with individual children and enter into those children's lives in a healthy, caring way.

The good news: God has placed those people in your church. There are people who are capable and willing—*if* you provide a vision for special needs ministry, coupled with a training program that volunteers believe will equip them to be effective.

Pray for those people. Pray that God reveals to them their place in special needs ministry.

Just for You

One thing about volunteers—they won't step forward and sign on to a ministry project until they trust the leadership that's provided.

That's you. You've stepped up to the plate and made it clear you're committed to your church's special needs ministry. And your love of the kids and families you'll serve is contagious—you'll soon see it mirrored in others.

God bless you for taking the lead. For broadcasting the vision. For setting the pace.

Dear God,

This isn't a ministry that one person can do alone for long. Please bring others to serve the children and families you love, children and families who need your loving touch, the church's support, and a kind word.

In Jesus' name, amen.

8. Case Study: The Life of a Special Needs Ministry

by Louise Tucker Jones

It was a big step for our little church. We were about to add an educational director to our staff of four—pastor, music minister, youth minister, and secretary. A welcoming reception was planned for Sunday afternoon, and I definitely planned to attend.

Bob and his family were friendly, kind, and cordial as one by one church members filed through the line. The pastor stood beside Bob in a show of support, smiling as if he had won some grand prize. Finally, I was face to face with Bob and quickly introduced myself before spilling out my all-important question: "Have you ever worked with people who have special needs?" Oops! The friendly banter stopped. The pastor was no longer smiling as I rushed on with my conversation.

"I have a son with Down syndrome and progressive heart disease, and it's my dream to begin a ministry to people with special needs. There are many families in our community who could benefit from such a program. Would you be interested in starting one here at Henderson Hills?"

I'm sure the pastor wanted to shove a piece of cake in my mouth, push me through the line, and say, "She's such a prankster!" But Bob looked at me with interest. Or it might have been concern, surprise, or shock. He finally said, "I'll think about that."

Then he added what I call his "casualty clause." He said, "Every time you see me in the hall, remind me." I agreed.

I was already teaching a Sunday school class for four-year-olds in hopes of mainstreaming my son, but it wasn't working. Our classes were large, and I had only one helper—certainly not enough for one-on-one time with a developmentally challenged child.

My son, Jay, wasn't comfortable because the other children couldn't understand him. One child asked what language he spoke. And even though Jay was six years old, the lessons were far too complex to hold his interest. He needed and deserved a class on his level. A class where he could learn about Jesus in his own special way. I was determined to get one.

Over the next months, whenever I'd see Bob at church, I'd say, "Just want to remind you of our need for a special ministry program." He'd turn, nod, and with a pitiful expression move through the crowd. I almost felt sorry for the man.

One Person Is a Ministry

Finally, Bob met with my husband and me and expressed his heartfelt desire for a special ministry program. His own daughter once contracted Epstein-Barr virus and had gone through intensive therapy. It gave him a small window into the world of disabilities. But there were problems.

"Who'll teach the class?" Bob asked.

"We will," I quickly answered, feeling certain we'd eventually find help.

"What about curriculum?" Bob asked. "There are no materials designed for people with special needs. How will you handle that?"

Having adapted everything from storybooks to Sunday school material, I had no qualms about this. I told him I could adapt lessons from an age-appropriate program and, if need be, write my own lessons.

Bob's questions continued: "What about students? Assuming there are families interested, how will you let families know we have a program?"

We did some brainstorming on that and came up with newspaper ads and a note to send home with children in special education classes at school. At that time the children were segregated into one building, and the administration allowed notes to go home with the kids. I also knew several parents that I'd call personally.

Finally, Bob sighed and delivered the final blow: "Even if you could find teachers, materials, and students, we have no room. There's not a single room available for another class."

My heart sank. There had to be *something*! Bob apologized. "Maybe in the future..." he said. But I wasn't going to be deterred.

"How about the storage room?" I asked. Bob nearly laughed as I continued. "It's large enough. Don't you have any other place you could put the teaching materials?" Bob shook his head. "Then we'll work around it," I announced. "Just give us a little corner to claim as our own."

"People come and go throughout the hour," Bob protested. "It's not a good solution."

Maybe it *wasn't* the best, but it certainly beat nothing—and I didn't back down. A few Sundays later my husband, son, one helper, and I met in the storage room with a cardboard box of supplies I brought from home, and we began a ministry.

Children's Ministry

I called every parent I knew. We put ads in the paper and sent notes home from school. I was certain every parent was as anxious as I was for a special class where their children could learn about Jesus. I pictured our little room quickly filled to the brim, but it didn't happen.

Weeks passed without a single student joining my son.

Finally, we gained one more young man. But by the end of the year, our growth hardly looked like a ministry to Bob; at least until I reminded him that we were the only Sunday school class that had doubled membership in one year. Bob couldn't argue with *that*.

In fact, he gave us a different room—a storage room on the *second* floor of the building! The advantage: It had a window and a lovely mural on one wall; the disadvantage: The room was *upstairs.* Thankfully, our two students could handle the climb, and we continued to pray for more children.

I realized that parents were skeptical. They didn't know if their children would really be accepted, or if we'd still be there next month. Some parents stayed home. Others had never gone to church.

Vacation Bible school opened a door. Again, I called parents and advertised in the newspaper that we'd have a class for children with special needs. It was summer, and many parents were desperate to find care for their children. Also, it was just a week, not a commitment for every Sunday. So we had four to six students attend, depending on the day.

Some of those students continued coming to our Sunday school class, and we finally reached an enrollment of five children.

Adult Ministry

About this time we had a wonderful young couple join our church who wanted to help in our ministry. Pam was a special education teacher, and Stan was a physician. Together they'd begun a special needs ministry in their previous church. God was blessing us indeed!

A few months later, our pastor received a letter about a young woman who'd moved to a group home in our town. She needed a church home. Stan and Pam brought her to church each Sunday, and soon a friend of hers also began to attend.

Suddenly, we realized we needed an *adult* special needs ministry, too. We started picking up adults at group homes on Sunday mornings, and our "bus ministry" was born.

But space remained an issue. The children had been moved downstairs into a tiny cubicle off the kitchen, then finally into a "real" room with a table, chairs, and storage for toys, books, and supplies. It was like heaven.

Stan and Pam taught the adults in a little house that had once served as the church parsonage. But that ended the morning that Nova Center, an intermediate care facility, brought a vanload of students without warning us ahead of time. Many of the students were in wheelchairs—which didn't fit through the parsonage doorway.

Thankfully, the fellowship hall had just been renovated into new classroom space, and we eventually spilled over into three rooms. We had students of all ages and abilities, even workers from the Nova Center who had never heard about Jesus. God had definitely dropped a ministry right into our laps.

Reverse Mainstreaming

As our adult group grew, our children's program dwindled. In domino fashion, the kids moved away, one by one, until we were back to two children.

Wanting more socialization and stimulation for my students, I visited a third-grade class in hopes of getting volunteers to come to our class for half of the Sunday school hour. I began by asking if there was anything that was especially hard for them to do, even confessing my poor math skills. Then I told them about our children with special needs who had trouble with everything—even talking, walking, and eating.

I asked if any of the third-graders would be interested in coming to our class as friends, not helpers. Friends are equal; helpers are not. Hands shot up all over the classroom, and for the next several months, two students at a time from the regular classroom came to our class and learned in the same way as our children.

We sang songs in sign language and told stories with puppets, pictures, and flannel boards. We pasted words on paper for Bible verses. Children loved it, and we gained a new special needs child.

I figured if I could change the attitudes of these third-graders about people with disabilities, they'd grow up with a healthy outlook about people with disabilities and influence their own peers.

One Sunday morning was especially revealing when one of our children became upset, and I didn't know why. The third-grade friend said, "Brian has his chair." Sure enough, when we switched chairs all was well. The third-grade friend had been attentive enough to see what had happened and understood his friend's speech.

Special Events

From the onset, our church reserved one Sunday evening a year for Special Ministry Sunday. On that night our students greeted people, gave out bulletins, sang songs, quoted Bible verses, said prayers, and took up the offering. We also had testimonies from parents, teachers, and even students.

One touching testimony was from Lee Ann, a young woman with Down syndrome. Her mother had taken her to church her whole life, but her father was not a believer. Lee Ann understood salvation and couldn't handle the thought that her father, who was quite ill, wouldn't go to heaven.

One day while her mother was away, Lee Ann sat beside her daddy, led him though the plan of salvation, and prayed with him as he accepted Jesus as his Savior. Her father died the next day. What an impact her testimony made on our members. There wasn't a dry eye in the auditorium, and many people's perceptions changed about challenged individuals.

We also hold a Christmas celebration for our students each year, complete with a full-course meal served by members of our church, professional photographs taken beside the Christmas tree, and special gifts. The students provide their own entertainment, getting on stage and singing whatever their hearts desire. It's their day to shine—and what a joy it is to bask in that light.

Programs, Problems, and Priorities

Of course, things haven't always run smoothly.

Many times we've been left out when mailings detailed the family programs our church offers to church members and the public. One VBS director assumed our little group would just sit in our room until I informed her we required a place in the auditorium, a time slot with the volunteer recreation team, and refreshments! It was years before a staff person took us on as a project and got us on the church budget. Materials, equipment, books, and toys were hard to come by, and space was at a premium.

But we trudged on in spite of the challenges.

Eventually we added other programs and events: a spring picnic in the park, a fall hayride, a summer conference, a teen class, an adult Bible study for advanced students, and a choir made up of people of all ages and different disabilities. Our choir has performed at several churches and at the Special Olympics in our state.

We also developed a special ministries team made up of parents, teachers, special education specialists, and staff members to help manage the programs. We have helpers for students who are being mainstreamed.

We also have an "extended session," staffed by volunteers, for older children who cannot go into the nursery or church service. One little girl is both blind and autistic, while another child has cerebral palsy and a trach tube. We have volunteer nurses rotating on a weekly basis with these medically fragile children.

We're hoping to develop a respite care program so parents can have at least one night out each month. Our Parent Connection, a support group, is open to the public and provides a nonjudgmental atmosphere where parents can air their frustrations, fears, and joys, as well as hear speakers on many topics.

Something More

Our little church where our special ministry program began in a storage room is now a church with over five thousand members. Now in its twentieth year, our special ministry program continues to grow, serving more than seventy-five individuals.

Our teachers and team members are called on regularly to help other churches start ministry programs. We feel privileged that God has entrusted us with these priceless and treasured jewels of his kingdom.

And it all started with one little boy named Jay!

9. Evangelizing Children With Special Needs—and Their Families

by Pat Verbal

I doubt anyone active in children's ministry will vote against this statement: It's important to help children know, love, and follow Jesus. Part of that process is helping children respond to Jesus' gift of love and his call to accept him as Savior and Lord.

That's a given. We create age-appropriate programs—Sunday school classes, children's worship experiences, midweek programming, vacation Bible schools—to help children know, love, and follow Jesus.

What's *not* a given is whether we believe that Jesus' invitation to children includes children with special needs. If someone were to judge a church by its programming, it might be easy to decide that in the minds of some churches, special needs children aren't part of the group Jesus came to reach.

But when special needs children—and their families—are shown the gospel in appropriate ways, they tend to draw near to God just as typical children and their families.

Imagine how a message of hope touches a family with a special needs child—a message of safety, wholeness, and value. Inviting families with special needs children to hear this message is like tossing a life preserver to a person who's drowning in a world of endless challenges and stormy seas.

special needs—special ministry
for children's ministry

And just as there are age-appropriate and relevant ways to help typical children know, love, and follow Jesus, there are appropriate ways to nurture special needs children to do the same.

So you've got to decide: Will you include *all* children in outreach and education efforts?

And helping a child know, love, and follow Jesus is more than bringing the child to a point of recognizing Jesus for who he is. It *also* includes helping each child find a place to serve in the church.

If you want to provide evangelism but not discipleship opportunities, you're missing the boat. Where will children who have special needs find a place to serve in your church? What opportunities will you provide?

The Apostle Paul reminds us that each member of Christ's body is important and has value. "The eye cannot say to the hand, 'I don't need you!' And the head cannot say to the feet, 'I don't need you!' On the contrary, those parts of the body that seem to be weaker are indispensable, and the parts that we think are less honorable we treat with special honor" (1 Corinthians 12:21-23a).

> If you want to provide evangelism but not discipleship opportunities, you're missing the boat.

So there are two questions you and your church must answer:

- *Do you wish to evangelize every child—including special needs children?*
- *Is there a place for every child to grow and serve in your church?*

I'm trusting that you'll enthusiastically answer yes to both questions and that through your leadership your church will share your enthusiasm for the evangelism of all children.

Embrace Relational Evangelism

My father had a homespun philosophy about life. He used to say, "Half the world takes care of the other half."

I've watched that happen. The people of God are often called on to be caregivers. It seems to be an important step to becoming soul winners. That's who we are; it's what we do. We tell others about our Jesus—one child at a time. We help families carry their cross—one family at a time.

It's our caring and our willingness to get involved that gives us credibility when we talk about the love of God expressed in Christ Jesus.

Remember that families of special needs children are often already stressed to the max. Everything they do—all the activities, relationships, and commitments—are viewed through the filter of how it will impact their children with special needs.

That's why to engage a family with special needs you'd better come with an understanding of the life they're living. And you'll find you won't always get a warm welcome. Unfortunately, families of children with special needs sometimes are resistant to churches and the message of God's love. And if you'd walk a few weeks in their shoes, you'd see why. Some of the obstacles you might encounter when reaching out to these families include the following:

Obstacle 1: the belief that God doesn't care

"It's not fair," cried Joshua, a frustrated second-grader who has dyslexia. "I get in trouble for things I don't know and that's just not right." His hot tears broke my heart. In utter frustration, Joshua often says, "I'm not dumb!"

We all assure Joshua he's right—he's *not* dumb. He's a smart, sweet, sensitive child who happens to have a learning disability.

Like Joshua, families with special needs children know that life isn't fair. So some of them figure God must not be fair either. Why then should they worship God or attend a church that honors God? God turned his back on them; what do they have to lose by turning their backs on him?

Words alone will never penetrate this attitude. It takes patient love expressed through action.

Obstacle 2: an insulated lifestyle

Well-meaning moms and dads, in an effort to protect their children, can become housebound, living a "cocoon" lifestyle.

In part, the family may be reacting to the difficulties associated with involving their child in a church. Depending on the disability, transportation and care might be major challenges. So might scheduling.

Or the insulation may be in reaction to the ridicule the child has endured at the hands of others. Finger-pointing, name-calling, and other emotional abuse can tear away at a child's esteem. Sometimes protecting the child from places where yet again the child can be misunderstood or mistreated seems the wisest course of action. And that might include church.

Obstacle 3: a crusading focus

Some parents can become "fighters" for the cause, living with a bitter spirit that assumes "normal" parents can't possibly understand their situation. These parents become angry at life in general and God in particular.

They push away or ignore relational overtures from organizations or individuals who don't live with a special needs child in the house.

These parents are crusaders, men and women on a mission. Unless you're willing to wholeheartedly join them, there's no room for you in their lives.

Obstacle 4: sheer exhaustion

When Jesus told us to take up our cross and follow him (Matthew 10:38), he knew we'd all have our share of troubles. They come with the territory. But crosses can become too heavy to bear alone. Even Jesus became so weary he dropped his cross. A man named Simon carried it for him (Mark 15:21; Luke 23:26).

There are few crosses heavier than watching one's child endure physical pain or emotional suffering. Multiple surgeries, barrages of medical tests and ongoing treatments, people pointing and staring…they take a toll as day after day parents grind on, juggling commitments and serving their children.

The hours are long. There are no days off. The pressure never lessens.

Then you come along with an invitation to come to a church service or a Bible study or to choose a faith that promises to demand more change, more time, more challenge. Small wonder these tired families don't jump on board. They're exhausted.

Obstacle 5: negative experiences with Christians

We church folk mean well, but our good intentions don't always translate well.

My friend, Chris, recalls a time that her son, Kenny, was in the hospital with kidney failure and a temperature of 105 degrees. She says, "I got a phone call at five in the morning from a church friend. I was so desperate to hold on to my son's life that I would have done just about anything at that point."

Chris' friend told her to call the hospital immediately. Her friend said that God had spoken to her in prayer and told her that Kenny had been healed. When Chris called the hospital, Kenny was worse, not better. "I was angry, not so much at my friend, but at the whole situation," Chris says.

On another occasion, church visitors to Kenny's hospital room told Chris it wasn't God's will for Kenny to die; if Chris prayed enough, he'd live.

In light of those experiences, how open do you think Chris would be to a message to join a church? To commit her life to a God who prompted a 5 a.m. phone call and found her prayers unacceptable?

Were Chris not already a believer, I doubt she'd be open at all.

Obstacle 6: the guilt factor

This obstacle is one that parents already attending your church may experience. They may feel as if they're a burden to you and your programs. As a result, they feel guilty and uncomfortable.

At many churches, members are urged to give time and energy to the ministries of the church. It's communicated in sermons, in bulletins and announcements, and in the tired eyes of current volunteers who need help.

But parents of special needs children often find their emotional wells are dry. Sunday mornings are an oasis for them. They often don't have the emotional energy to serve in leadership—*especially* in children's ministry.

Yet they appreciate the special needs ministry you're providing. They know what a blessing your ministry is to them, and…they see that you need help. The result: guilt that they're not more involved. Guilt can prompt parents to not attend church. So be intentional about letting these maxed-out parents know that you want to serve *them*. They can relax and be refreshed while their children are in programs at your church.

How do you overcome these sorts of obstacles and reach these families with the gospel? Easy: You do it in the same way God intended you to share your faith with *anyone:* through building loving relationships that give you permission to speak into the lives of people who need to hear about Jesus.

> The more you understand the world of a family with a disabled child, the more you'll be heard when you share the gospel.

That's *not* to say that God can't use a crusade, revival, or a door-to-door witnessing team to bring the gospel into the lives of families who have children with disabilities. God can use any means he wants to accomplish his will.

But in general, the more you understand the world of a family with a disabled child, the more you'll be heard when you share the gospel. That's because you'll be sharing it in a context that makes sense to the family and the child.

I've found that sometimes families and their children will get involved in a church program or event even if they don't have any previous experience with churches. That's because the event is one of very few planned for children with special needs.

Here are some ways you can reach out to the community, with an eye toward forming relationships with families. These "evangelism events" are each designed to engage and support families with special needs children where they live and breathe:

Host weekly support groups for parents, caregivers, and siblings.

You'll need a place to meet and a means to advertise. And may I suggest that though you'll be tempted to lump all three of these groups into one support group, it's good if you keep them separate. Why? Because someone in the family has to stay home to care for the special needs child. And because the issues for a parent may be very different than the issues faced by a sibling.

And, of course, you'll need to have a competent facilitator available.

Provide "respite care."

On a monthly (or bimonthly) basis, host an event where children with special needs are dropped off at the church for the evening and parents get the chance to dine out, shop, or simply rest. In providing this much-needed break, we model the body of Christ and open the door to helping others know him.

You'll need to have sufficient volunteers and an appropriate program prepared. This sort of event can quickly create "regulars" in the community who become familiar with your volunteer staff and facility.

Provide a family night for churched and unchurched families.

Families with special needs children want opportunities for their children to make friends, play with typical children, and enjoy socializing in a safe, accepting environment.

You can provide that opportunity by hosting a regular evening of programming in which families with typical children are invited to have fun alongside families with special needs children. Have families share a meal, play games, and simply interact.

But be sure the families with typical children know that special needs children will be there. And one church I'm familiar with is growing because they hand out fliers at a large school for the blind each month.

Hold a family retreat or camp.

Family retreats and camps are the highlight of many families' annual vacation. Relationships are built that change lives, especially for those who go to serve, not to be served.

I've heard people who've organized this sort of camp report that parents consider their family retreats a slice of heaven on earth. Why? Because the camps were places the entire family felt understood, at home, and supported.

Host seminars that build parenting and marriage skills.

The strain of raising a child with special needs can seriously challenge a marriage. Provide practical support by holding regular seminars that don't require a long-term commitment or an ongoing scheduling challenge.

Plan outreach events that serve the special needs community.

One church hosted a spring fashion show and luncheon featuring "adaptive apparel." They worked with a clothing retailer that specialized in garments that are easy to get into if a person is in a wheelchair or wears leg braces. They invited a community leader who was also disabled to emcee the event, and 125 people attended.

Create plays that include roles for special needs children.

Stories like Max Lucado's *The Crippled Lamb* and *You Are Special* make great plays. Young children are born actors and love dress-up. Ask your church drama team or a talented individual in the congregation to adapt a favorite story for children with disabilities to perform on stage. Invite everyone to try out, and include anyone who cares enough to try out.

Party! Party! Party!

Find or create a reason to throw a party. The Royal Hearts Club I directed in Yorba Linda, California, had an annual '50s party. At first I wondered, *What do these kids know about the '50s?* But their parents helped girls dress in poodle skirts and bobby socks. The boys sported black leather jackets with their hair slicked back in ducktails. Children jumped at the chance to imitate Elvis Presley as "golden oldies" blasted through the sound system. Our attendance doubled, and parents had as much fun as the kids.

Note: Everyone looked "different" because of the dress-up. There was no need to feel self-conscious about a cleft palate or leg braces. Not when the kid standing up front had paste-on sideburns!

Embrace Evangelism That Helps Children Grow in Faith, Love, and Knowledge of God

You've reached out and have families with special needs children involved in your church.

Now it's equally important in the evangelism process to provide places for those children to grow in their faith and to express their faith in service. It's not enough to "warehouse" children as you serve their parents and siblings. The special needs children God has brought to you deserve to grow too.

Encourage growth in the classroom.

Children have a great spiritual capacity to know God, but they need instruction—just like adults. In many churches that instruction takes place in Sunday school and is delivered by talking.

Lectures and talks simply won't work well with many special needs children (or typical children either!). That approach assumes a level of language comprehension a child may not possess. Or lectures may simply be beside the point: What the child needs is to feel the love of Christ expressed through relationships, and lectures don't encourage relationships to form and flourish.

The goal of a class isn't to cover a lot of material; it's to communicate with children in a relevant way—to come alongside children and encourage those who don't know Jesus to experience him, to help children who know Jesus to love him, and to help children who love Jesus to actively follow and serve him.

Generally speaking, there are several things to consider when adapting Sunday school curriculum for use in a special needs classroom:

1. Relax. Good teaching is good teaching for all children.

Effective ministry to kids is effective ministry to *all* kids. If leaders are sensitive to each child in their care, they'll make many accommodation adjustments automatically. Encourage leaders to focus less on how they're teaching and more on whether children are engaged and learning. A learner-centered approach to teaching makes sure no child will be left behind.

2. Know your children.

Talk with parents to discover...

- Whether children have special equipment, such as wheelchairs, and how the area can be best adapted to accommodate such equipment.
- If you know physically challenged children will attend the program, make sure your classroom is wheelchair accessible.

- What kids can and cannot eat, including foods that cause allergic reactions.
- Specific medical assistance children might require.
- Specifics about what children need help doing and what they want to do for themselves. It's important not to stigmatize children, in spite of physical or invisible limitations. The rest of the kids will take cues from the teacher about how to treat individuals with disabilities. If the teachers communicate love and sensitivity, it will be imitated.

3. Ask leaders to be open to adjusting their teaching in these ways:

Greater attention. Children with disabilities often need extra help to participate in activities. Ask an additional person to serve as a peer mentor or a "buddy" of a child with disabilities. This allows teachers to continue distributing attention equally amongst the class.

Greater persistence. When working with children with learning disabilities, lessons may require extra explanation. When leaders give one instruction at a time, they should use positive-language suggestions and praise even the most minor achievements. It will help children with disabilities take pride in their accomplishments. Simplify activities and instructions, but don't patronize or talk down to students with special needs.

Greater frequency. A teacher may need to establish limits, review rules, or reiterate instructions more often. In these instances, it's best to repeat shared information to the entire group to benefit all the children with reinforcement.

> The goal of teaching isn't to cover ground as you dash through the Bible lessons on time.

Remember: The goal of teaching isn't to cover ground as you dash through the Bible lessons on time. The goal is to nurture young faith and establish it in willing, loving hearts. Some children with special needs will never be able to memorize the books of the Bible in order. Other children with special needs could easily bury you in a game of Bible trivia. Don't assume that an impaired ability to see or speak implies impaired capacity to learn.

Encourage growth through service.

I'm tempted to suggest that you invite children with special needs to participate in whatever service projects typical children in your church do...except many churches don't let children—typical or with disabilities—serve at all. Children are observers. They're kept on the bench, watching the action until at some point in the future, they're called into the game of service.

Are there tasks that a child in a wheelchair can't do? Absolutely. But there's not a service *ministry* the child can't do. If a child has a desire to help others, to be used in a ministry of helps, there's something for that child to do.

It probably won't be helping to shovel the driveway of a senior adult who's unable to do the job. But how about calling and encouraging that senior or writing a cheerful card? Absolutely! That's ministry—and that's service a child in a wheelchair can easily do.

So let children serve—in meaningful ways—and you'll help them grow.

Surround special needs children with "faith-enablers." These are the sort of adults who...

- Act in ways that communicate they believe special needs children have a dynamic faith experience and can know, love, and follow Jesus.
- Authentically listen to children, aware that God can speak to and through them.
- Are careful not to belittle or put down children.
- Include children in spiritual activities along with adults.
- Are willing to see and respond to children as people rather than disabilities.
- Trust God to use special needs children to do significant and meaningful ministry.

What are service projects that a child with special needs could participate in? Here are some suggestions:

- *Adapt whatever service programs already exist to make room for children with special needs.* Do you have a children's choir? a puppet team? How could you expand those ministries to include children with special needs?
- *Involve children as greeters or ushers.* There's no one who can deliver a heartfelt handshake and greeting quite like a young man with Down syndrome. And you'll send a message to each and every visitor: Everyone is welcome here.
- *Recruit children to pray for staff.* I'm convinced that God listens to children! Ask children to each "adopt" a church staff member for a day to pray for that person. Let the staff member know the child is praying for him or her.
- *Ask the child what he or she enjoys doing, and turn it into a service project.* If children have made a faith commitment

Evangelizing Children With Special Needs

and know God, they have been gifted to serve. In what ways? Ask children what they enjoy, what they do well, what they want to do. Then find ways to provide opportunities for them to serve.

- *Encourage children to make gifts for others.* It can be colorful finger-painted pictures for shut-ins or bookmarks for the church library. What's important is that the project is meaningful and truly helps someone else. "Busy work" doesn't build self-esteem.

- *Ask children to volunteer in a resource center.* If you have a centralized area for keeping craft supplies and curriculum resources, let children keep it neat and organized. You may need to provide very attentive supervision, but it's certainly a significant service project. And there's a bonus: As teachers pick up supplies or drop them off, there's a chance for your students to hear a sincere thank you from adults they've served.

- *Ask children to be custodial helpers.* They can empty trash, wash white-boards, and clear off tables.

- *Ask children to help with food.* If your church has a Wednesday night family meal or a snack table on Sunday morning, children can set tables, help serve food, and make table centerpieces.

- *And don't forget the church office.* Children can help with folding or stuffing bulletins; their help will be welcome. If your children are ushers, they'll be able to quickly make the connection between how they served the church office staff and how they're serving visitors and members of the congregation.

Remember: Evangelism is a process. It may take time.

We like to see results. We'd like to share the gospel one time and see a child's eyes light up with understanding and commitment. But in the same way that it's often not the case with adults, it's often not the case with children who have special needs.

For instance, consider Alex.

A public high school teacher stopped me in the hall one morning after Sunday school. Judy's eyes rimmed with tears as she told me about her nephew, Alex.

"My sister called this weekend and wants us to take Alex," Judy said. "He's on medication for hyperactivity and behind in school. When he

special needs—special ministry
for children's ministry

stayed with us last summer, I worried that he was being neglected because he was so thin." Alex's mom struggles with mental problems requiring hospitalization. "We want to do what's right for Alex," Judy continued. "But Jeff and I have our own two sons to think about. How will bringing Alex to live with us affect them?"

We talked about Judy's fears. As she made preparations to become Alex's legal guardian, provided him health insurance, and enrolled him in school, I prayed for God's guidance in Alex's future.

More than anything else, Jeff and Judy wanted Alex to learn to trust Jesus through this difficult time. "I know Alex must be thinking that his parents don't want him," Judy sighed. "How sad is that!"

Learning to trust Jesus and developing a healthy sense of self weren't going to happen overnight. The process of accepting Jesus was going to take time. It was going to require the patient, loving example of Jeff and Judy. And being accepted and welcomed into church would certainly help, too.

> You build the kingdom one child at a time, and each child has unique needs.

Don't be discouraged if the attendance of the special needs ministry never explodes like the attendance of the singles or youth ministries. You build the kingdom one child at a time, and each child has unique needs. In the case of special needs children, those needs can be significant.

But that's all the more reason to reach out to those children and their families—and reach out now.

Remember my friend Chris?

Her son, Kenny, was born with spina bifida. He had partial movement in his arms, but no movement from his chest down. Caring for him in a church setting was a challenge.

Yet Kenny's delightful personality always won peoples' hearts. Kenny loved Sundays and knew Jesus.

"Kenny thrived on the attention he got at church," says Chris. "Even though he wore an oxygen mask, no one seemed to shun him. Normal kids were fascinated by his sense of humor."

When Kenny died at the age of twelve, Chris was grateful for the church family, a family who celebrated Kenny's life.

I've discovered that children with special needs have a below-average life expectancy. They live a little more on the edge. They tend to have less robust immune systems and more medical complications than typical children. Parents of these children are aware that their children are at risk.

Often, the children know it too.

These aren't children we can set aside to evangelize later in life. There may not *be* a "later in life" for them. If they're going to hear about Jesus and serve him, now is the time.

Do you value evangelism?

Do you value the worth of each child?

How would the family of a child with disabilities be able to tell if they walked into your church next Sunday morning?

Just for You

Jesus wants children to come to him—to know, love, and follow him.

He valued all children. So do you. He reaches out to everyone—the great and small, the rich and poor, those who run swiftly, and those who are crippled and lame. You're reaching out to everyone too.

You're doing the work of God. Rejoice in that! Celebrate the obstacles and difficulties you encounter—they're reminders to lean on God for strength as you serve him.

Dear God,

Bring the children into our ministry you want here. Give us grace to greet them all the same way you would greet them.

In Jesus' name, amen.

10. How to Partner With Community Agencies

by Pat Verbal

It's an annual challenge around my house: When November rolls around, I start hearing hints about how wonderful it would be to have a traditional American Thanksgiving meal. A turkey with all the trimmings—and that includes everything from homemade cranberry dressing to fresh pumpkin pie with whipped cream topping.

Of course, never in all the time I've heard these hints has it ever been mentioned that anyone wants to help me prepare this meal. The cooking (and cleaning, too!) is supposed to be *my* contribution to the holiday. The *rest* of the family's contribution is to watch football and compliment me on the meal.

There was a time I dragged out recipe books and started a two-page list of all the ingredients I'd need. It was just assumed I'd whip everything up from scratch, and I didn't want to disappoint anyone.

Those days are long gone, believe me. I can still baste a mean turkey, but I've caught on that almost everything I need for Thanksgiving dinner comes either in a ready-to-go box or is frozen in a bag.

We're all busy; all looking for quicker, easier ways to get things done. It's not that I love my family less; it's that I simply don't have time to peel the potatoes, smush the cranberries, and preheat an oven two days in advance. I want to partner with Sara (Lee) and save myself some work.

And there's another reason I want to team up with someone else: I never *have* been able to make some of those recipes turn out right. I want to take advantage of Betty (Crocker) and her expertise.

There's no sense reinventing the wheel; that's my motto.

That philosophy applies to ministry, too. There are clearly times you have to start from scratch—creating programs that address unique needs in your community or church. Though even then you can probably learn a few things by seeing how other churches approach similar issues.

> Sometimes it pays to cooperate. And it always pays to learn from others.

I live in Texas. We don't have lots of youth groups organizing snow-shoveling service projects down here. Any youth group that wants to put one together will have to figure it out from the ground up. Around here, that's a start-from-scratch ministry.

But if you're put in charge of a swim ministry (Don't laugh. There are swim ministries in churches where lots of kids go to camp or swim in area lakes), that's a good time to team up with a local community swimming pool. Arrange to rent or use the pool during certain hours and during that time teach the Bible lesson as you also teach kids to swim. For a swim ministry, you don't have to rip up the church parking lot and put in an Olympic-sized pool.

Sometimes it pays to cooperate. And it always pays to learn from others.

Special Needs Ministry as a Cooperative Effort—a Caution

You're starting a special needs ministry or moving yours up a notch. Nobody knows better than you that you can use a little help. I'd like to suggest partnering with both national organizations and with community agencies.

But first, a word of caution about partnerships.

Your goal as a ministry isn't just to improve the quality of life for special needs children and their families. That's a worthy goal, but not a uniquely Christian one. At some point you'll want to present biblical truth and invite people to have a relationship with God as well as with you. It's at that point you cross the line as far as many disabilities-related community agencies are concerned.

Agencies are often very willing to work with faith-based organizations like your church so long as you leave the faith stuff out of it. They're secular agencies, often funded through sources that strictly forbid discussing

special needs—special ministry
for children's ministry

faith issues. Even the Christians working at these agencies find their hands are tied.

When you partner with agencies, you run the risk of being "unequally yoked" with an organization that has very different goals than yours. What's deceptive is that you'll look like soul mates at first: You both care about special needs children, you both want to provide support and respite for parents, and you both may use the same language.

Ask the hard questions at the front end: What are your expectations regarding our sharing the gospel? about praying with people? about encouraging participation at church services?

There are excellent partnering opportunities out there, but not every opportunity is a match. Be open about your own intentions, and ask good questions about a potential partner's intentions and expectations.

And even if you can't find a local agency or two to serve as your partners, you're not alone. There are excellent Christian organizations that have experience, expertise, and a willingness to help.

Here are a few you'll want to contact.

Joni and Friends

Some moms and dads of children with disabilities feel the same way about Joni and Friends as you might feel about oxygen: They can't imagine life without this ministry. From the time their children were diagnosed with physical disabilities to the day they decided on living-assisted group homes, Joni and Friends ministry has been there to provide information, counseling, camps, retreats, and lots of love.

For over twenty years, Joni Eareckson Tada, from her own wheelchair, has reached out to disabled children and adults, family members, and friends.

Following a diving accident in 1967, Joni was left with no feeling from the neck down and only limited movement of her hands. In those early days of depression, Joni remembers the support of her church. She says her church friends made all the difference.

Joni says, "The darkness was lifted when friends from my church rallied around my family, offering help, hope, and ascribing positive meaning to my affliction. It was the church that kept us connected to reality, opening doors of possibilities and paving the way for me to re-enter the mainstream of life."

What could have happened if members of Joni's church hadn't opened their hearts and acted on the biblical call of Christ? Small wonder Joni has made it her life's work to train the church for effective ministry in the area of special needs.

Joni and Friends area ministries are teams of dedicated people who are willing to "get in the trenches" with your church. At the time of this printing, there are local offices in ten cities, but the ministry's reach is far broader through radio, correspondence, by mail, and through phone consultations. The radio program *Joni and Friends* is a five-minute broadcast hosted by Joni and is carried on more than five hundred radio stations daily.

Joni and Friends is probably the largest and best-known national special needs ministry and a great resource to visit on the Web. You'll find print resources, training opportunities, and a sweet, caring spirit. Add www.joniandfriends.org to your "favorites" list—you'll stop by often.

Through the Roof

Through the Roof is a ministry based in the Dallas/Fort Worth area, but it partners with churches throughout America. Director Robert Durbin explains the unusual name of the ministry by pointing to Mark 2:3-4, a description of how four friends helped a paralytic reach Jesus by lowering the man through a roof.

This ministry, which is an affiliate of Joni and Friends, provides the following:

- Assistance for disability ministry coordinators in developing disability ministries within their churches.
- Support in maintaining and expanding disability ministries in the church and community.
- Resources to help equip churches to provide more effective disability ministries.
- Training for disability ministry coordinators in developing and equipping volunteers.
- Networking of churches and disability ministry coordinators, facilitating meetings, and training opportunities.
- Partnering to provide opportunities for church disability ministries to participate in program activities, training, workshops, and events hosted by Joni and Friends, successful churches, and other organizations.

Sound like an organization that could be of help to you? For a list of churches in their network, check www.joniandfriends.org and www.throughtheroof.org.

Break the Barriers

Another friend of churches serving children with disabilities is located in Fresno, California.

I first encountered the Break the Barriers team at a meeting for children's pastors in Denver. The nine hundred pastors in the audience expected to see a show put on by some handicapped kids, but this talented troupe of athletes far exceeded that expectation.

An eight-year-old blind girl tumbled through the air. Young men with Down syndrome carried on their shoulders smiling children in wheelchairs as red, white, and blue streamers waved to the rhythm of upbeat music. We quickly forgot about the disabilities of the athletes and began to envy their sheer talent and joy.

> We quickly forgot about the disabilities of the athletes and began to envy their sheer talent and joy.

And that's the point.

When Break the Barriers' founder, Deby Hergenrader, was a little girl, she enjoyed gymnastics and playing baseball. It frustrated Deby that her sister Kathy wasn't allowed to participate because Kathy had Down syndrome. So Deby and her brother started a sports club in their back yard where all children were welcome.

"Little did I know how God would use my sister, Kathy, in my life," says Deby. "In 1983 I asked God to help me show the world that all people belong together. That's when I started Break the Barriers, a nonprofit public facility serving all faiths and cultures."

Since 1983 Deby and her husband, Steve, have ministered to hundreds of families and led an amazing team that performs more than fifty times each year. Their organization works with churches and schools to use events to draw attention to a need for working with the special needs community—in a fun way.

"My mother always said you can't beat people over the head to get them to accept children and adults with disabilities," says Deby. "But you can throw a party and hope they'll want to be part of it...that's what we do every day at Break the Barriers. I believe my sister, Kathy, was created perfect and has all she needs to fulfill the purpose God put her on earth to serve."

Break the Barriers offers a full range of consultation services to help you start and maintain an effective special needs ministry in your community. You can reach them at www.breakthebarriers.org or (559) 432-6292.

Mephibosheth Ministry

This organization, based in Colorado Springs, Colorado, provides consultation to help churches accept, evangelize, and equip children and adults with special needs. Ministry founder Mary Jane Ponten shares a powerful testimony.

"As a person who looks quite out of the ordinary because I was born with cerebral palsy, my life could be full of frustration, fear, and hatred—but for Christ. I accepted Jesus as my Savior in my first year of college, though I had been raised in a Christ-centered home and a good church. The uniqueness of my life and the way God has used me in so many areas of his service, has prepared me to see the potential we are wasting in the body of Christ as we ignore the service of those who are also 'out of the ordinary.' "

> "My life could be full of frustration, fear, and hatred—but for Christ."

You can reach Ms. Ponten or ministry co-founder John Nix at www.mephibosheth.org.

Any of these national resources are yours to tap for the price of a phone call or an online visit. See what services they provide and how the emphases of your ministry line up with theirs.

Working With Schools

How many teachers do you know? How many teachers are in the public elementary school closest to where your church meets?

Now multiply that number by two.

You'll be hard pressed to find a teacher who doesn't have at least two children with special needs in his or her classroom and who wouldn't welcome assistance in making the education process a success for each of those children.

What would the impact be if your church provided five volunteers per week to a special education teacher at your local school? If once every day, someone showed up to provide help? It would be huge. Trust me. I've seen it.

You can't overestimate the impact of caring Christians volunteering to serve special needs children in a local school. And the impact is not just on the children themselves. Teachers who have their loads lessened, even for a few hours per week, feel the difference. Families whose children get some desperately needed attention and tutoring feel the difference, and the teachers at church will feel the difference too.

When I'm helping a child with disabilities at church, I ask for the parent's permission to visit the child's school. Spending even half a day with that child in a classroom environment helps me more than any general training I could take because each child's situation is unique. This is *especially* true for children with severe physical disabilities.

I watch how the teacher handles the child's needs. Sometimes teachers expect more of a child than parents expect, and I can see how a child functions when doing his or her absolute best. Teachers are often better able to describe a child's social interaction because parents tend to be alone with their children and don't see peer-to-peer social interactions.

I'm careful to call in advance, follow school procedures, and take notes to refer to later. I'm respectful of the school's process, and I remember to thank teachers and school administrators. Those courtesies go a long way in smoothing the way for me to return later.

Here's a real-world example of how connecting with a local school has helped one church's special needs ministry...

When my friend Ramero was in elementary school, he found it difficult to read. That disability made for a difficult time in school, and Ramero desired to connect with similarly challenged children so he could assist them.

Sharing his dream with fellow church members, Ramero recruited several children's ministry volunteers to serve as mentors in a local school. After passing the required background checks, they were each given the opportunity to visit a child once a week.

The mentors met together at church on Sundays, encouraging each other and praying for the children they served. It wasn't long before word traveled into the community that Ramero's congregation cared deeply about children with special needs. Several families began to attend the church, and a teacher from the school became a member of the church.

> Word traveled into the community that Ramero's congregation cared deeply about children with special needs.

Something to keep in mind: Dealing with special needs professionals requires a specialized language. Like all specialists, therapists and teachers have developed their own vocabulary, and the meaning of words won't necessarily be evident to nonprofessionals. Get in the habit of asking questions and taking notes.

Here are a few terms with which you'll need to become familiar:

Adaptive behavior: the extent to which a child is able to adjust to a new environment, task, object, or person

The Regional Preschool Training and Technical Assistance Project provides information for educators and parents of disabled children ages three through five. Professional training, staff development, evaluation, and conference information is included in a publication, the LEEP Network News.

There's also a Family Talk section that provides practical activities for parents and children.

Contact: LEEP, Human Development Center, LSUMC School of Allied Health Professions, 1100 Florida Ave., Building 180, New Orleans, Louisiana 70119.

Assistive technology: any equipment or systems used to increase function with children with disabilities

At risk: children who are likely to have difficulties due to home or medical circumstances

Due process: a formal session between parents and schools conducted by an impartial officer to resolve special education disagreements

IDEA: Individuals with Disabilities Education Act or "appropriate" educational plan to meet a students needs

IEP: Individualized Education Program written for each child in special education

Least Restrictive Environment (LRE): placement of child with disabilities in a setting with maximum contact with children who do not have disabilities (mainstreaming)

Related services: services students require to get special education, transportation, counseling, speech therapy, and crisis intervention

Screening committee: the local school committee who decides if the child qualifies for special education

Self-contained class: children with disabilities have their own class

Service coordinator: the person who works with child, parent, school officials, and social services

Working With Social Services

Throughout history, babies born with obvious disabilities didn't fare well. They usually either didn't survive or were immediately institutionalized.

Today with advances in medicine and education, many of today's fragile children are raised in loving homes until they reach adulthood. Still, even parents who have the best of intentions can become emotionally, physically, and financially drained. When this happens children may be placed in foster homes, government funded group homes, or given up for adoption.

That's when government social service agencies get involved.

It's easy to criticize any government agency, and often social services agencies are represented in the media as callous or uncaring. In my experience, nothing could be further from the truth. I've yet to encounter a social services representative who's uncaring. Representatives are often overworked, carrying caseloads that make success difficult. Social services offices are often underfunded and understaffed. And they're often bound by red tape that could make a bureaucrat scream. But they're not uncaring.

So see them as potential allies, not enemies.

In many churches across the country, you'll find one or more foster families. You don't need to request a list from social services to find these folks. They have a strong word-of-mouth communication system, and they know fellow-caregivers who might be struggling. Pray for ways to connect with foster families that are on the front line of caring for special needs children, and watch how God will work.

Consider being intentional about linking with state and regional organizations that serve children with disabilities and their families. One quick way to locate agencies and organizations in your area is through a Web search. The relevant sites change frequently, but at the time this book went to print, one of the best is www.childrenwithdisabilities.ncjrs.org/states.html.

Ask parents of children with disabilities for help connecting with grassroots consortia in your area that offer parental support and resource networks. These are excellent places to distribute fliers and other information announcing your ministry.

One source for agency connections that may be open to you is through local colleges or universities. Check with the staff in the college of education. Professors who work with special education courses are often highly networked and know what agencies are serving your community. While you're on the phone, ask for an appointment. Use that time to share your vision for your church, and ask how you and the college might partner. Are there students who would like to do unpaid internships? Is there research that the professor wants to conduct that wouldn't interfere with your program—and might bring some resources and grant money flowing in to fund your efforts? How can you connect with agencies that might want to know about your program? Be open to connections that might develop as you stay in touch.

> You can expect God to use people as your ministry develops.

It's helpful to have already created a mission statement and defined your goals before you explore partnering with agencies of any sort. Again, the outcomes you desire may overlap but not be ultimately compatible. If accepting a grant to outfit a special needs classroom in your church requires you to give up presenting the gospel, the price is too high.

You can expect God to use people as your ministry develops. Consider what happened with Susan…

As Susan searched for a job, she ran across an ad in the paper advertising for a "child advocate" in the court system. It was a volunteer position requiring four weeks of training in order to learn how to visit children in foster homes, and then act as a spokesperson during court proceedings.

With three busy children of her own and a need for a paying position, signing on for a volunteer role didn't seem like a solid career or economic move. Yet God seemed to be speaking to Susan's heart. After a few weeks of prayer, she went for an interview and began training.

It was during this time Susan's church decided to start a special needs ministry that would reach out to the community. No one could have predicted how Susan's new job and this new ministry would dovetail so beautifully. No one but God, that is. Many of the children she served had behavioral and learning disabilities. Her free training and firsthand contact with needy children provided much needed help at church.

Who is God using to interact with special needs children and their families through the courts in your town? Tell them what you're doing. God may bring about a partnership.

Another church planned a holiday party to serve foster families in their community. Children at the church made invitations and decorations, purchased gifts, and baked refreshments for the party. They led games and were intentional about welcoming and including children with special needs from the foster families that came to the party. Then the church kids prayed for the visitors and the needs of the foster families.

Who is God using to interact with special needs children and their families through foster families in your town? Tell the people in that agency what you're doing. God may bring about a partnership there, too.

> **If you want to reach people, it helps to go where they are.**

A women's Bible study had met for ten years with little change until one woman's grandchild was placed in a nearby group home. Out of love for their friend, the women in the Bible study volunteered to take turns visiting the home. They soon discovered how much they looked forward to seeing the children. They also realized they were making a difference, and the whole dynamic of their Bible study sessions changed.

Who's visiting the children in group homes? Tell those people what you're doing, and watch for partnerships to form there, too.

Working With Community Events

If you want to reach people, it helps to go where they are.

For many families with special needs children, several events have become regular highlights. Having your ministry volunteers actively involved provides a great opportunity to build a relational bridge between your ministry and families in your community.

Have the Olympics come to your town lately?

Many churches encourage their members to get involved with local Special Olympics. This international organization is dedicated to empowering individuals with mental retardation to become physically fit, productive, and respected members of society through sports training and competition. Special Olympics offers children and adults with mental retardation year-round training and competition in twenty-six Olympic-type sports.

Currently, one million people with mental retardation participate in Special Olympics through more than two hundred programs in 150 countries. By 2005, Special Olympics hopes to double the number of athletes involved to two million. Children and adults who participate improve physical fitness and motor skills, develop greater self-confidence, and enjoy a more positive self-image. They grow mentally, socially, and spiritually; and enjoy the rewards of friendship.

The goals of the Special Olympics don't specifically include participants knowing, loving, and following Jesus, but time spent serving and meeting special needs families is time well-spent. You'll help your volunteers build a greater heart for the developmentally disabled and also forge relationships.

Help the children at your church learn about the Special Olympics through a free curriculum available at www.specialolympics.org.

Host a basketball team.

If your church has a gym, you can partner with the National Wheelchair Basketball Association. It has a junior division and offers five national camps plus a Junior World Championship playoff. With 190 teams nationwide, there are other teams to play and an opportunity for children in wheelchairs to still get some hoop action.

The good news: Many typical basketball teams have a team chaplain. Provide that service for the team you host, and you'll have weekly opportunities to invite children and their families to your church when the gym is used for worship instead of basketball! For more information, check out www.nwba.org.

Help shape other events.

Your community probably has dozens of golf tournaments, fun runs, craft fairs, neighborhood theater presentations, holiday parades and picnics, art shows, and concerts. Find out who organizes them, and make someone from your ministry available to help the planners see those events through the eyes of someone with disabilities.

It's likely that adapting the event so it's accessible to children with special needs won't take much—except for intentional inclusion. If your approach is gentle and helpful rather than shrill, you'll find there's an interest in cooperating.

Become known as an advocate for special needs children not just in your church but also in your community. If your church has a passion for helping families with special needs children that extends past your church walls, you'll be perceived as truly interested.

Working With Group Homes

Like most parents, Lynn and Larry Tremel expected their daughter to grow up, move away from home, and have a family of her own.

Nineteen years ago they knew that would probably never happen. At five months of age, Megan failed to thrive and by age three she was diagnosed with multiple mental and physical disorders, including mental retardation, epilepsy, and cerebral palsy. As her body grew into womanhood, emotionally she kept her preschool mannerisms.

"Megan walks and talks," says Lynn. "She's very social, but not highly teachable. She's not interested in learning how to dress herself, brush her teeth, shave under her arms, or take a bath." Naturally, Lynn and Larry are concerned for Megan's future. Emotionally, they've yet been able to visit a group home for Megan.

The Tremels are like many parents facing retirement years with an adult special needs son or daughter.

"There's a school in Wichita, Kansas, that teaches life skills to young people like Megan. We're going by there this summer on our vacation. I'm praying about sending her there before we consider a private group home nearby."

The Tremels are like many parents facing retirement years with an adult special needs son or daughter. Although Megan has older sisters who'll look after her, their parents don't expect them to take her into their homes.

"We've taken legal action to become Megan's adult guardians, and set up a living will for her care," says Lynn. "We don't want to put Megan in a group living facility just because we're getting older. We want to do it because it's the best thing for Megan."

Many group homes are privately funded Christian facilities. These homes long for the support of local churches in their community. You can partner with them by holding worship services at the home or offering transportation to your church's services or special events. Your church can join in fund-raising efforts and provide counseling for parents, siblings, and grandparents.

LuAnn Ruoss keeps in contact with group homes in Bakersfield, California, where she's director of special needs ministry at the First Presbyterian Church. "I've learned that it takes time and patience to build relationships. Some people are defensive toward the church because they've been treated so badly," says LuAnn. "I've tried to be consistent and do all I can to show how much we care. Now, the directors call me when a resident needs assistance moving to a new place. I get a group from church, and we get the job done."

Don't be discouraged if any community agency is less than receptive at first.

Identify the group homes in your community. Set up appointments to find out what they need and how open they are to your involvement. Let the group home suggest what a partnership might look like and, as LuAnn suggests, be willing to move slowly. Trust takes time.

Don't be discouraged if any community agency is less than receptive at first. Especially if they've seen church special needs ministries come and go, they may be hesitant to depend on you for consistent involvement. It's important not to make promises you can't keep. If you can't reliably provide transportation to your church each Sunday, say so. It's better to follow through on a monthly commitment than fail to keep a weekly commitment.

And if you need a vision for why partnerships can be a thing worth pursuing, keep in mind these words from President George W. Bush:

"When governments, business and individuals work together, to build a welcoming society, Americans of every ability will benefit" (June 19, 2001).

That's true, you know. There's tremendous benefit in not reinventing the wheel, not reproducing services that are already available. By working with or alongside existing agencies, other churches, and willing community groups, you can expand the scope of your ministry without having to build everything from scratch. And you can concentrate on doing what you do best, what you bring to the mix that's unique and valuable.

Just for You

Reaching out into the community can put you in contact with people who don't share your values or goals. That's OK—that's part of being salt and light in the world. What counts is that you're there giving of yourself. That you're there listening. That you're there ready to serve.

Thanks for initiating relationships that God can use in powerful ways. Pray daily for God to work in his time and in his way to bring opportunities for your ministry to connect with special needs kids and their families.

> *Dear God,*
>
> *Thank you for the chance to be your ambassador in this world. What a privilege! Bless the efforts of our special needs ministry and protect our hearts.*
>
> *In Jesus' name, amen.*

11. Case Study: The Wrap-Around Model—A New Opportunity for Children's Ministries

by Larry Shallenberger

I live in Erie, Pennsylvania. Like many towns across America, our town struggles with children who live in poverty. The outlook for children *twice* cursed—with both poverty and mental health issues—is doubly bleak. These children are likely to experience school problems, abuse, and violence.

Every month, a team of social workers, psychologists, and pastors sit around a coffee table and plan how to address the needs for some of Erie's neediest families. A few decades ago, a mutual distrust would have prevented these disciplines from meaningful cooperation: Pastors, social workers, and psychologists seemed like strange bedfellows. But shifts in philosophies in these fields have created a new common ground.

A Tale of Two Mattresses

The ancient Greeks told the story of Procrustes, a host who took pride in his hospitality and his abilities as a fastidious host. He set a splendid table but had one quirk: Overnight guests were measured against the length of the guest bed. A torture rack stretched smaller guests until they fit the length of the mattress. Procrustes literally cut long guests down to the size of the mattress with a handsaw. Procrustes valued having guests fit his mattress. His guests wished he'd valued fitting the mattress to them instead.

Both churches and social service agencies have at times had a "Procrustes Complex." We want people to conform to programs rather than adapting programs to fit people.

In church settings, we invest hundreds of hours in creating top-flight programs for kids and families. Most families and children comfortably fit on "mattresses" of programming. However, some families just don't fit no matter how much we push and pull on them.

Consider the Jones. The Jones family consists of Mary, a single mom, and eight-year-old Jerry. Mary dropped Jerry off at Sunday school and joined an adult education class. Halfway through class, Jerry made grunting noises and grimaced his face uncontrollably. A half dozen redirections later, the teacher became visibly annoyed and demanded that Jerry stop his disrespectful behavior. The other kids in class snickered. Jerry didn't fit in—and he knew it.

After class the teacher pulled Mary aside and vented her frustration about Jerry. Mary considered explaining that Jerry has Tourette's syndrome, but she didn't trust the teacher's willingness to empathize. Besides, she felt out of place in her Sunday school class too. She was the only single parent in the group, and the class was halfway through a thirteen-week series on marriage.

College kids made up the bulk of the singles class, so she didn't fit there either. The Jones never came back. The Christian education director threw his hands in the air and cried, "Church hoppers!"

Mary fumed as she wondered if *anything* in life truly fit her family. Jerry's probation officer got angry with her for not cooperating with a treatment plan. Juvenile probation appeared after Jerry skipped a dozen days of school, preferring the comfort of his video game system to the constant heckling awaiting him at school.

Mary hadn't noticed Jerry's truancy in her scramble to make ends meet. She was too busy working at Wal-Mart and the adult health club. She hated what she did for a living and hated the fact that the probation officer kept a record of her employment in Jerry's file. The judge ordered her to attend parenting classes, but she was usually working one of her two jobs. If she did get time off, she couldn't find a baby sitter willing to watch Jerry.

Mary could almost guarantee Jerry would skip school whenever she was scheduled to work at Wal-Mart, but Mary felt powerless to stop it. The probation officer informed her that at the next court review, he was recommending foster care for Jerry due to the family's lack of cooperation.

The Jones family tried to fit into a church's programming—and failed. And that happens more than we may want to admit. Today's families are too diverse, too injured, and too broken to fit a one-size-fits-all model.

special needs—special ministry
for children's ministry

The Goldilocks Principle

There's another folk tale involving a weary traveler and lodging that provides a healthier model of ministry: *Goldilocks and the Three Bears.*

The Goldilocks Principle is this: When given choices and protection from predators, the weary traveler will eventually find a meal, a chair, and a bed that fits "just right." But it won't be the *same* meal, chair, and bed for each traveler.

The Goldilocks Principle is based on common sense. As a treatment philosophy, it's best described by the "wrap-around" model, and it surfaced in the social service field through the work of Canadian John Brown. Chicago's Kaleidoscope program adopted wrap-around principles in 1975. In 1985, Alaska adopted the model under consultation from John Van De Berg. Since then, over thirty states have attempted to reproduce the model for service providing.

Here are the principles in a nutshell. How well do they describe how you're providing service and programming for special needs children in your church?

Needs Orientation Versus Service Orientation

The foundation for deciding how to help a family is by asking the family what it needs. Too often we attempt to channel everyone into our existing programs. But if a family won't benefit from those programs or simply can't make them work, we can save everyone frustration by understanding that upfront. Then we can decide how to respond.

Strength-Based Versus Deficit-Based

Traditional treatment plans focused on what the family was doing wrong. Once upon a time, a family would sit at the table and hear professionals label them dysfunctional, enmeshed, or chaotic.

Professionals labeled children with tags like hyperactive or conduct disordered. The child assumed that since he or she was in trouble that these big words meant "bad."

If we apply wrap-around planning, the child and family team identifies strengths the family can draw on as they set out to become healthier people. Strengths include cultural heritage, interests, and character traits the family values. Any intervention the team proposes must have a clear connection to the strengths of the family. Otherwise, it doesn't enter the treatment plan.

A church's special needs ministry can be integral to comprehensive planning rather than a sidelight or afterthought.

Holistic Versus One-Dimensional Focus

Wrap-around planning touches all domains of life including the extended family; living environment; financial stability; educational/vocational strengths and weaknesses; social behavior; emotional, psychological, and physical health; legal issues; and safety. Traditional plans centered only on problem behavior and ignored the rest of the child's life.

By ignoring the child's real world, churches and service agencies discard the possibility of motivating the child through intrinsic means. Tell children that you want to work on their antisocial behavior and their eyes glaze over. Ask children if they'd like to learn how to make and keep friends at school, and you might get their attention.

Cultural Competency Versus Cookie-Cutter Conformity

Wrap-around planning acknowledges that every family has its own unique culture consisting of its values, traditions, preferences, and history.

Great wrap-around plans embrace what the family *already* values. If a family embraces Christianity, then the planning team must make sure that faith plays a real role in the child's treatment. This "cultural competency" value creates countless opportunities for the churches to minister to a new segment of families, provided churches are prepared and interested...and that they're willing to work with social agencies.

Balanced Versus Formal Supports

Supports available to families fall into two categories—formal and informal resources.

Formal supports include services that public and private insurance can bill, such as therapy or psychiatric appointments. Informal supports cannot bill insurance companies. The YMCA, a neighbor, Uncle Bob, community recreation programs, and local churches are all informal resources.

Before wrap-around emerged, the power informal resources possessed in providing long-term support was ignored. However, the change in philosophy coupled with shrinking state budgets have encouraged mental health professionals to include informal resources in their treatment planning. An ideal treatment plan involves a balance of both formal and informal resources. An at-risk child needs specialists, but family and community remain long after therapy sessions end. This paradigm shift is causing many county mental health systems to recruit churches to participate in providing services for children.

How Wrap-Around Looks at Grace Church

Grace Church became involved in wrap-around planning in 1998. I'd recently left my position as a case manager at a local mental health residential treatment center to become the children's pastor at Grace. I was invited to serve on the Community Resource Team of the Erie County Wrap-Around Office. The Community Resource Team was founded to help identify informal resources for the families of children experiencing severe mental health issues.

Most referrals the team handled were requests to address family's basic needs. Frequently, survival needs prevented families from finding the energy to address their emotional needs. Grace's volunteers responded by providing used furniture as well as car and home repairs for the families.

Referrals grew at a staggering rate. Our youth ministry, under the direction of Derek Sanford, founded Target Work Camps. Our teenagers worked at several homes in the inner city, tackling everything from patching drywall to installing aluminum siding.

Our children's ministry added a Target Adventure Camp as a way to meet the emotional and spiritual needs of children. During the same week as the Target Work Camp, we opened our doors to children involved in wrap-around services. We planned the programming, and local mental health professionals donated their time to provide clinical support. Children learned basic social skills, such as anger management, from a biblical point of view. They also learned living skills such as nutrition and cooking.

Infrequently, a family became interested in Grace and began attending the church. *This* was the challenging part. Addressing a physical need with money and labor is simple. Providing spiritual support for the families within the limits of our programming has been more difficult, but that's where the wrap-around planning is invaluable.

Meet the Smiths

The Smith family lives near Grace Church in a housing development. Jenny, the mother, has chronic respiratory problems; she is raising three children on a fixed income. Her health problems require frequent hospitalizations and prevent her from holding a stable job.

Jill, the youngest, had trouble in school and was diagnosed with a seizure disorder and hyperactivity. Jill had angrily punched several holes in the walls of her house, and Jenny was unsure how to discipline her.

Jill receives mobile therapy and has a therapeutic staff support person, who provides one-on-one supervision so Jill can get through the school day. Jill's caseworker referred several home repairs to the Community Resource Team, so a Target Work Team visited the Smith's home to start the repairs. Teams of volunteers from the church completed the projects, and one volunteer befriended Jenny and Jill.

Soon Jill was attending Sunday school, and Jenny began attending church. Through the women's ministry, Jenny paired up with a mentor who helped her develop spiritually. Jenny receives occasional financial support and car repair. Grace Church's business administrator has helped Jenny design a budget. Jenny attended a spiritual gifts course and is now a volunteer at Grace's kitchen and in the youth ministry.

Jill attends Grace Church sporadically. However, Jenny has learned parenting skills from the mental health provider, and the church has helped her provide loving discipline for Jill. Jenny has a new set of coping skills that benefit her daughter.

Meet Victor

Victor has Asberger's syndrome. Asberger's is a mild form of autism that prevents its sufferers from easily picking up social cues. Victor was not involved in the community mental health system, but the wrap-around philosophy provided a road map for meeting Victor's needs.

Victor's parents were concerned that Victor couldn't adapt to the junior high youth group. Throwing Victor into a crowd of adolescents going through their own emotional and hormonal transitions would have been a high-risk decision.

Meetings with Victor and his parents revealed he loved helping younger children. Victor became a helper in a preschool classroom.

The plan wasn't perfect. After a team meeting with Victor's psychologist, his parents, Victor, and me, we realized that the size of the preschool class overwhelmed Victor. Some of the children knew that Victor was different and asked Victor questions. The children sometimes called him names. Victor needed help processing his feelings toward the children. We agreed to let Victor help at a different service with fewer children. The psychologist shared that Victor needed to have more concrete responsibilities so he could understand his role in the classroom.

After two years Victor decided to no longer work as a helper. Instead of entering a power struggle with Victor, his parents created a plan that didn't involve our children's ministry. While Victor is no longer serving in this capacity, the process helped him discover his spiritual gifts and talents. The team defined Victor by his strengths, and he's welcome to return to children's ministry whenever he chooses.

Embracing the Wrap-Around Model in Your Special Needs Ministry

This model of working with children who have special needs provides you opportunities—but probably only if you seek them out. Here are some first steps you might take if you want to get involved.

Connect

Seek out local social service agencies, and discover if there is a Community Team that your church can join. Ask if there are any gaps in services that your church could fill. When you come across a child in your church who's in the mental health system, let a parent know that you'd be happy to sit in on the next child and family meeting.

Check Your Current Systems

Are your safety, screening, and recruiting systems in place and working well? If you welcome special needs children, they'll come. Be ready.

Check Your Training

Your volunteers will need to be extra prepared to handle discipline issues. Train your teachers to turn to the family for answers when they're unsure how to work with a child. Develop a culture that values creative solutions over ejecting a child from the classroom.

The wrap-around model isn't about building new programs. Rather, it's about building a new process that honors families before flowcharts. Welcome the surprises and challenges that come from touching families! Eventually you'll hear a special needs "Goldilocks" say, "This church is just right."

12. Facility and Liability Considerations

by Pat Verbal

*"I rejoiced with those who said to me,
'Let us go to the house of the Lord.' "*
—Psalm 122:1

Perhaps you think of David when you read this familiar psalm.

I'll never see it again without thinking of Katherine and Jim Harrison.

The couple and their daughter, Jenni, had relocated to Plano, Texas. They were anxious to find a church home, but couldn't find a place where Jenni's needs could be met.

Jenni was deaf, and like many people who are hearing impaired, she couldn't read sign language.

Surprised? Don't be. Many people with hearing impairments easily follow what you're saying in conversation—they read lips fluently. But that's of little help in a church sanctuary where the speaker is far away from most of the audience.

Katherine and Jim were so frustrated they were considering giving up on church.

There was a time when any church with a sign language interpreter was considered a community leader in special needs ministry. Today the ideal solution for assisting those with a hearing loss also includes something called captioning. It works like closed captioning on television.

A typist, often a court reporter, enters every word that's spoken into a computer with special software. The text is viewed on a TV monitor that can be seen by the congregation.

Most of the churches the Harrisons visited didn't have a viable program for the deaf but expressed an interest in putting one in place—someday. The problem for the Harrisons was that Jenni was there *today* and needed integration *now*.

That's when the Harrisons found Prince of Peace Lutheran Church in Carrolton, Texas.

"Jenni was the catalyst," said Rev. Stephen Wagner in a story reported in the Dallas Morning News. "We were presented with a need that was right in our face...We'd done some research. We knew that if we could put together a ministry for the hearing impaired that we would meet a need in our community."

The technology—called a CART program—is expensive and has been slow to catch on, but it's a solution that works with any hearing impaired person who's able to read. That includes not only people who are deaf, but also people who are older and have sustained hearing loss. Anyone who can follow along as text moves across an elevated screen is able to benefit.

> It doesn't take a total hearing loss for church members to be unable to understand what's said in a large auditorium.

The Harrisons were able to be—all three of them—fully involved in worship.

Creating Friendly Facilities

A computer software program, video screen, and fast typist probably weren't the first things you thought of when it came to turning your church sanctuary into a space that's friendly for a special needs ministry, but it could be that simple. At least for churches that are seeing the average age of their membership creep upward, a program like the one that helped the Harrisons may be inevitable. It doesn't take a total hearing loss for church members to be unable to understand what's said in a large auditorium.

For children with mental or emotional disabilities, your current classrooms are probably already equipped to meet their needs. What needs to be adapted may be your teaching style and lessons. Children—and adults—with physical disabilities will be most affected by the limits of your church's physical facility.

Something to Bring Up at Your Next Building Committee Meeting

All new building construction is required to meet standards set by the ADA, as are buildings that are used for community meetings. If your facility is used as a preschool or school or if community groups use it for meetings, you have to be ADA compliant.

If your church building is old, updating it to meet the standards described below may be nearly impossible, no matter how large the budget. Still there will be items on this list you *can* accomplish—perhaps by taking advantage of skills already in your congregation.

Pull together a meeting with qualified craftsmen who are in your membership. Be clear that attending the meeting will in no way commit them to donating the materials or labor needed to make all the modifications on the list. Rather, you're asking for the help of these professionals and skilled amateurs to determine what can be done, what it will cost, and how to get the most bang for the buck.

You need this information. And you may discover that your team catches the vision and chooses to step up and do some of the work. Be sure to include others on your facilities tour, too—several people who currently use walkers, wheelchairs, and canes, for example. They're valuable consultants.

Brainstorm with the church finance committee once you know how much money a partial or complete renovation would require. What funds are available? What means are available for raising funds from the church or community? What are the obstacles in your way?

Do What You Can Do

It's easy to look at your aging facility—built when ADA was but a distant dream—and wonder how you could ever turn steep stairs into a wheelchair friendly entrance. It's easy to think, "Well, we'll just change the facility when we build a new building." So the changes are put off for another year...or decade...or longer.

Don't worry about changing everything. Instead, do one small thing, and let the momentum build from there. Even a handrail where one didn't exist before will draw attention—and give you an excuse to celebrate with a ribbon cutting. Let people see that even if it's a slow process, your church is moving toward taking steps to include people with special needs.

One of the churches I worked with took three years to add an elevator and crosswalk that connected two educational buildings. If you think that sounds like a long time, you've missed my point. It's this: The people advocating for children with special needs didn't give up. It took three years, but it happened.

Another church carried children's wheelchairs up and down the stairs every Sunday. Members of this church couldn't afford to renovate, but they could afford to have some smiling faces and sturdy backs on hand to welcome children with special needs anyway.

Whatever your facility challenges may be, God already knows about them. He looks at your church's heart, and that's where accessibility really begins. With God's help—and your nudging—that heart is a space that can be renovated and redecorated to welcome all children in Jesus' name.

Following is an excellent guide developed by That All May Worship and the National Organization on Disabilities that will help you evaluate your church's facility. How are you doing at providing a facility devoid of these barriers?

Facility Barrier Audit

Parking and Paths

- ☐ Curb cuts to sidewalks and ramps to building entrances
- ☐ Pathways at least 48 inches wide, with a slope of no more than 5 percent
- ☐ Level resting spaces of at least 5x5 feet around doors
- ☐ Marked accessible parking spaces close to accessible entrances

Ramps and Stairs

- ☐ Ramps at least 36 inches wide, extending 1 foot in length for every inch of rise, a 1–12 ratio. (A ramp replacing an 8-inch step must extend 8 feet.)
- ☐ Nonskid surfaces with handrails on at least one side of ramps
- ☐ Ramps reasonably protected from rain and snow
- ☐ Stairs with handrails on both sides—handrails 32 inches above step and extending a foot beyond top and bottom of stairs

☐ Stairs with rubber treads

☐ Slightly raised abrasive strips on top steps to warn people with limited sight where stairs begin

Doors and Doorways

☐ Door openings 32 inches wide or more

☐ Doors which can be opened by exerting five pounds of pressure

☐ Doors which can be opened electrically by the push of a button

☐ Lever handles or push bars on doors

Worship Space

☐ Seating space with extra legroom for people using crutches, walkers, braces, or casts

☐ Scattered spaces or "pew cuts" for wheelchair users who prefer to be seated in main body of congregation, not in front or back of sanctuary and not in aisles. (Pew cuts can be easily made by shortening several pews by 36 inches.)

☐ Area with lecterns and microphones need to be accessible to those with mobility impairments

☐ Choir seating arranged to accommodate wheelchair so wheelchair users can participate

☐ Adequate lighting directed on face of speaker so those who read lips can do so, and adequate general lighting in sanctuary

☐ Bookstands or lapboards available for those who are unable to hold prayer books, hymnals, or Bibles

Bathrooms

☐ At least one accessible bathroom, ideally one on each floor. These may be unisex, such as those found in airplanes or homes

☐ One toilet stall 36 inches wide with 48 inches clear depth from door, closing to front of commode, and a 32-inch door that swings out

☐ Ideally, 5x5 toilet stall with a 32-inch door that swings out and two grab bars, one adjacent to commode and

one behind commode, to facilitate side transfer from wheelchair

☐ Hospital or shower curtain providing privacy for wheel-chair users, if metal dividers are removed and other renovations are not possible at the moment

☐ Sink with 29 inches of clearance from floor to bottom of sink

☐ Towel dispensers no higher than 40 inches from floor

☐ Lever-type faucet controls and hardware on doors

Water Fountains

☐ Water fountain mounted with basin no more than 36 inches from floor and easily operated from wheelchairs

☐ An interim measure: supply of paper cups mounted next to water fountain or water cooler

Elevators and Lifts

☐ Elevator or chair lifts to ensure access to sanctuary and all major program areas

☐ Controls placed at 54 inches or less from elevator floor, reachable from wheelchairs

☐ Broiled plaques on elevator control panels

☐ Handrails on at least one side of lift or elevator, 32 inches from floor

How to Comply With ADA

Not everyone reading this book will be in America, so please forgive the constant references to American law. If your church is elsewhere, by all means work to comply with your own standards.

But the process described below will probably be useful whether you're in Canada, England, or India. Adapt it as necessary.

1. Plan ahead.

The time to take federal, regional, and city codes into consideration is at the front-end of any new building project or building renovation. A mistake or oversight made on a planning sheet or blueprint can be easily corrected. Once construction is underway or finished, modifications are remarkably expensive.

Determine to meet every standard. Hold yourself accountable, not only because the building inspector will, but because barriers you fail to remove *in* your facility will work to keep people who need to be a part of your fellowship *out*.

2. Do your homework.

Obtain copies of the ADA requirements, and give them to your architect and building contractor. These construction professionals will probably already be familiar with the requirements, but you want to be certain. You want to be sure that you and the construction professionals are on the same page when one of you says, "Let's make sure we meet the requirements." If you're working from the same document, there won't be surprises halfway through the project.

Be up to date on emerging technologies that might impact how you deliver services to special needs children. You may need to have more electrical outlets and more circuits in rooms that might have medical monitoring equipment that travels with some children. It's less expensive to make electrical and plumbing accommodations proactively rather than after the fact.

3. Be clear about your priorities.

Most church building programs are an exercise in compromise.

The worship team would like a full soundboard that's the envy of any recording studio; it eventually settles for six microphones and a mixer. The counseling ministry wants a suite of offices that presents a professional image; it eventually is happy with better soundproofing and a reception desk.

It's easy to get lost in the process unless it's absolutely clear that no matter what other compromises are struck, compliance with ADA regulations is non-negotiable. Ask your architect to provide written confirmation that building plans and construction drawings comply with all ADA requirements.

And be sure that your legal counsel includes contractual terms in design and building contracts that require your architect and building contractor to fix and pay the costs of any construction that does not meet ADA standards. Once the facility is constructed, reconfirm that the facility meets all ADA requirements during a separate walk-through just for this purpose.

4. Be your own watchdog.

During construction or remodeling, keep an eye open for common mistakes. Local officials usually review construction planning documents to

make sure that state and local building and fire-code requirements are met, but they often aren't authorized to enforce federal laws like the ADA. Consequently, if they sign off on blueprints and you OK them as well—assuming that ADA concerns have been monitored—you might well be assuming responsibility for any ADA oversights yourself.

I'm not implying that construction professionals deliberately try to cut ADA mandated accommodations from building projects. I'm saying that even a simple construction project is a labyrinth of details, and unless someone is specifically looking out for ADA interests, it's easy to make mistakes. Anyone who's survived a home kitchen remodeling project knows how complex even a small project can become; imagine putting together a church building!

Keep an eye on the ADA construction issues you and the contractor have agreed to build into the project. Make sure they're still there—at every checkoff built into the construction process.

5. Show up and wander around.

Here's your chance to wear a hard hat! You've been a watchdog, but nothing beats showing up and checking in now and then. Most ADA mistakes occur in the building design, but many occur during the construction process. ADA mistakes that occur during construction can often be avoided if an architect or an ADA consultant visits the construction site and monitors progress to make sure the building is being constructed according to plan. Don't be afraid of paying a few dollars to hire a professional to do this once or twice.

> **ADA Materials Available From the Department of Justice—Free!**
>
> The U.S. Department of Justice provides free ADA information and materials in these formats: standard print, large print, audiotape, Braille, and computer disk for people with disabilities.
>
> **Phone**—Call the ADA Information Line 1-800-514-0301 (voice) or 1-800-514-0383 (TDD). Automated service is available for recorded information and to order publications.
>
> **Fax**—The automated fax system is available twenty-four hours a day. To order a publication by fax, call the ADA Information Line and follow directions for placing a fax order.
>
> **CD-ROM**—Order ADA regulations, design standards, and technical assistance documents on CD-ROM from the ADA Information Line or at www.usdoj.gov/crt/ada/adahom1.htm.

6. Follow through, follow through, follow through.

Inspect completed work carefully. Identify mistakes and take action to have them fixed. And do it not *just* because it's the right thing to do.

The Department of Justice is responsible for enforcing the ADA and ADA enforcement at newly constructed public buildings. Private individuals may file complaints about inaccessible facilities with the department, or they may file their own lawsuits in federal court alleging ADA violations at facilities. Don't find out the hard way if ADA applies to you in your new facility—

be diligent, and ensure complete ADA compliance so you won't upset any prospective visitors who have disabilities.

Liability Considerations

As children's leaders, we take the health and safety of all children very seriously. Provisions for children with special needs are probably covered under your church's general liability insurance, but it's good to check with your church's insurance provider and legal counsel. You might want to take care of this *before* meeting with a church leadership team to recommend creating a special needs ministry; it's a question that might come up.

Some programs ask parents to complete liability release and care forms that clearly state children will be cared for by nonmedically certified volunteers. Using this sort of form makes sure the parents know exactly what level of care you can—and can't—provide. It's clear and helps manage expectations.

Do *not* imply that you have trained medical professionals available if it's not true. That you have a licensed therapist or pediatrician in the congregation who's probably in the building on Sunday morning does *not* constitute attending staff. Parents of special needs children need to know what they can expect from you as you care for their children. Let them know completely and accurately; they'll appreciate your candor.

If you use release forms, present them in as loving a manner as possible. Be sensitive; some parents have been turned away by Christian educators when parents disclosed information about their children. Your goal isn't to scare parents away but rather to communicate your desire to prevent emergencies and give the safest, highest-quality care possible.

While forms are fine, one-on-one conversations are even better. Talk with parents about their children. Give parents the opportunity to share their hearts as well as medical information. These parents know how to fill out forms; they've completed hundreds of them. But your focus is on more than a child's diagnosis. Use the check-in and background time to communicate your love for each child to the parents and to minister to parents themselves.

Please also know that no permission or authorization form makes you immune to lawsuits. If your staff and volunteers are negligent in the care of a child with special needs, it's exactly as if they were negligent in caring for a typical child. Negligence is negligence—there's no excuse for it whether or not a permission slip was signed.

Your goal is to gather information, provide better care, and enhance relationships that God can use to build bridges. Having paperwork signed is important, but it's not an end in itself.

Your Form Should Include...

- ☐ Usual contact information: child's name, age, address, e-mail address, and date
- ☐ How to reach parents at home, work, in the church building, and on their cell phones
- ☐ Space for the parent to identify the specific disability diagnosis or diagnoses
- ☐ Child's level of communication skills: speech, reading, writing, or sign language
- ☐ Brief history of child's response to separation and play with others, plus anything the parent(s) feel is important for you to know
- ☐ Name and phone number of child's primary physician
- ☐ Known allergies—to foods, drugs, and insects, for example
- ☐ Information concerning assistance the child might require—with food, hygienic needs, and sleep, for example
- ☐ Information regarding common behaviors—fears the child experiences or seizures, for example

In the interests of being comprehensive, you might also include the following authorization/release language. This is especially important if you'll be caring for children in a respite-care setting, where parents aren't in your facility as you care for children.

Be mindful that you'll want your insurance provider and/or legal counsel to review any forms you create.

Sample Authorization/Release Language

I have fully disclosed to _____ [name of your church] all pertinent facts about my child(ren)'s special needs, and I accept full responsibility for failure to do so. I understand the volunteers and staff want to provide the best possible care for my child, and I've done all I can to help them meet that goal.

If my child is enrolled in the respite program, I authorize the staff to provide any required special treatments or procedures to my child while in respite care. I will provide written authorization, instructions, and all necessary supplies and equipment for these procedures.

In case of an emergency or accident, I understand that the _____ [name of city] Emergency Medical Services (911) will be called. I authorize EMS to administer any medical treatment, medication, or appliance deemed necessary by the EMS. I also authorize transportation by EMS to the nearest appropriate medical facility, as determined by EMS. I understand that I will be responsible for payment of all EMS, hospital, and physician charges for emergency services to my child.

I have read and initialed the above permission/authorization statement and agree to the terms designed in each.

Signed: _____

(Parent/Guardian)

Date: _____

Just for You

Initiating or expanding your special needs ministry is risky. All the funds you need may not appear. All the volunteers you need may not sign up. Most of the families and children you want to serve might greet your grand efforts with a mighty yawn. After all your work, maybe just one child will respond.

That's success.

One child is worth it all. One soul. One family touched with the love of Christ expressed through a caring church.

Pray for the numbers you want to respond to your special needs ministry. Ask God to send you enough families and children that you're always and ever slightly overwhelmed. That keeps you depending on him.

But remember: One child is worth it all. One child is enough.

Dear God,

Thank you for the chance to serve special needs children and their families. For the opportunity to communicate your love through word, touch, and smiles. Thank you for knowing the names of every child who we'll touch. We can't wait to meet them and serve them as you've served us.

In Jesus' name, amen.

13. Sermons for Your Pastor

by Jim Pierson

A Letter From Dr. Pierson

Dear Pastor,

Since the late 1960s, I've spoken for many churches and conferences, encouraging listeners to open their hearts and church programs to people with disabilities and their families. In doing so, I've used several sermons. The following four are my favorites.

"Uniforms of Love" encourages Christians to show that they care about people with disabilities by following some practical suggestions. After preaching the sermon, I've frequently heard, "I can do those things. Thank you for making it so easy."

"At His Feet" reviews how Jesus responded to people with disabilities in his ministry. It also outlines what churches typically do and explores what churches and individuals in the audience *could* do.

"The Accessible Great Commission" drives home the point that everyone, regardless of ability, needs easy access to God's love through Jesus. The term *accessibility* is a well-known disability concept. The basic interpretation of accessibility is physical—how to negotiate a building with ease. However, in the Christian world, it also means *spiritual* accessibility.

"Faith, Friendship, and Disability" is my personal favorite. Referring to the well-known story of how four friends brought their friend with a physical disability to Jesus for healing, this sermon stresses the importance of friendship in helping people with disabilities get to *and* actively join in the life of a congregation.

Because of my years of experience working with many wonderful human beings with disabilities, I've incorporated their stories as illustrations in these sermons. I'd urge you to substitute your own illustrations from the lives of people you know, so your sermons ring true and you speak with passion.

The statistics presented in these sermons were accurate at the time of publication but may have changed. Double-check by using the Internet.

I share these outlines hoping they'll serve you well as you lead your congregation in embracing ministry to—and with—those who have disabilities. As these sermons and your own Bible study will confirm, there's a rock-solid biblical foundation for special needs ministry.

So please—adapt these messages as you will. Add to them. Delete what's not appropriate for your church at this time. Use them any way you can to present this truth: God loves people with disabilities. He welcomes them into his kingdom. We can do no less than to welcome those same people into our churches.

Sincerely,

Dr. Jim Pierson
President, Christian Church Foundation for the Handicapped
Knoxville, Tennessee

Uniforms of Love

Scripture Reading: John 13:34-35

Introduction

God's plan for getting his love to people is simple: He sent Jesus to demonstrate his love. Before returning to his Father, Jesus left instructions:

"Go into all the world and preach the good news to all creation" (Mark 16:15). And then there's this: "By this all men will know that you are my disciples, if you love one another."

God's plan is us. *We* wear the uniform of God's love. Just as emergency professionals wear instantly recognizable uniforms, the Christian's uniform of love should be equally as obvious. The fifty-four million people with disabilities in America need to be able to approach a loving Christian and expect a positive response. Let's talk about how we can communicate love to people with disabilities.

1. Respond to the person, *not* the disability.

- React to the person with cerebral palsy, not the cerebral palsy. David's brothers saw a spoiled younger brother. God, because he looks at a person's heart, saw a king of Israel.
- Instead of reacting to the hand movements and poor communication skills of a person with autism, a uniform wearer will see the potential of sharing the enriching love of Jesus.

2. Look at the person.

- When we make eye contact with someone, we acknowledge that person's presence. Do keep in mind that staring is one thing, giving a friendly look is another.
- Whether you're in a shopping mall, grocery store, or at church when you encounter a person with a disability, notice. A friendly smile from someone wearing the uniform of love encourages acceptance and lifts the spirits.

3. Touch the person with a disability.

- Touching suggests friendship. Jesus touched people who were blind, deaf, mentally ill, and who had leprosy.
- A touch from someone wearing the uniform of love can cut through the isolation some people with disabilities feel.

4. Do ordinary activities with the person who has a disability.

- Get to know the person's world—school, family, and daily schedule.
- Send a birthday card or other special-day card. Communicate that you're aware of the other person's world—and it counts to you.

- Share your life with the person who has a disability. Be open and real.

5. Encourage the person's family.

- Families are forever changed by disabilities. Disability is a *major* stress on marriage.
- Respite is a major need.
- There are four times of predictable crisis for families experiencing disability: when the diagnosis is given, when the child starts school, when school is over, and when parents realize they cannot provide care. Be there for families at these critical times!
- In Mark 9:17-27 Jesus showed sensitivity when he asked a young father (whose son the disciples couldn't heal), "How long has he been like this?" Jesus encouraged the father simply by engaging and recognizing the child's existence.

6. Share Jesus.

- People with disabilities are more *like* people without disabilities than they are *different* from people without disabilities. They have souls, which need to be nurtured by God's redeeming love.
- Even people with mental retardation and other developmental problems can be taught the message of God's love.
- Encourage your church to start a disability and special needs outreach. In doing so, you'll be welcomed as someone who wears the uniform of love.

Conclusion

God's love is important to all of us, regardless of ability. People with disabilities need to know about Jesus. As a wearer of the uniform of love, share the message of God's wonderful Son, Jesus, with people—including people with disabilities. Doing so makes an eternal difference.

At His Feet

Scripture Reading: Matthew 15:30-31

Introduction

As a believer in the Lord Jesus Christ, I'm required to love people. And as long as those people look like me, think like me, talk like me, and cheer for the same football team, loving is easy. But when the people are different, the "love everybody" directive is harder to manage.

Today I want to talk about loving people whom I'm required to love—even if they're different than me. People with disabilities need the love of God's people too.

People with disabilities were a major part of Jesus' ministry. Recognizing his concern, people with disabilities flocked to Jesus.

In today's Scripture passage, we learn that people with every kind of disability were brought to Jesus and "laid...at his feet." That makes sense when we note earlier that "he went up on a mountainside and sat down."

Let's explore how Jesus responded to these people with disabilities, how society responds, how the church responds, and what we as individuals can do when people with disabilities are presented to us.

1. How did Jesus respond when people with disabilities were "laid...at his feet"?

- He dealt with individuals.
- He involved the person in the plan. Jesus asked a man with a physical disability if he wanted to be healed (John 5:6) and a man who was blind what he wanted Jesus to do for him (Mark 10:51).
- He touched people with leprosy (Matthew 8:3).
- He thought helping people was better than following arbitrary rules. The Pharisees were furious when Jesus healed a man with a shriveled hand (Mark 3:1-6).
- He was sensitive to the families experiencing disability. He asked a young father how long his son had been disabled (Mark 9:20-24).

2. How does society respond when people with disabilities are "laid at its feet"?

- American society, primarily through the legal system, has opened up to people with disabilities.
- Since 1975 a mandatory education act has required every school system to provide a free and appropriate education for every child regardless of disability.
- In 1990 the Americans with Disabilities Act has made it easier for a person with disability to ride a bus, make a telephone call, and have a job in the community.
- Special Olympics demonstrates what people with disabilities can achieve.
- The media portrays people with disabilities as valuable.
- It would have been great had the church led the way with these initiatives, rather than the legal community.

3. How does the church respond when people with disabilities are "laid at its feet"?

- The situation is changing—for the better.
- An increasing number of churches are making their Sunday school programs inclusive by having a trained assistant accompany a child with a disability in Sunday school, children's church, and other programs.
- Families with children with disabilities are offered respite care.
- More seminars, training materials, and information in general are available to assist churches in starting disability ministries.
- The church is doing better by the disability population.

4. How do you respond when people with disabilities are "laid at your feet"?

- We're not suggesting that a person can necessarily be healed of a disability, but we can provide "healing" with a positive attitude toward the person.
- We can look at the person instead of turning our heads.
- We can greet the person instead of walking by or altering our path.
- We have an awesome responsibility. We become our Lord. We are his hands, eyes, and feet. We need to treat people with disabilities as Jesus treated them.

special needs—special ministry
for children's ministry

Conclusion

Can we do any less than follow Jesus' example when it comes to responding to people with disabilities? The fact is that *all* of us are tangled in sin that we can't escape.

The Accessible Great Commission

Scripture Reading: Matthew 28:19-20

Introduction

People with disabilities were often recipients of our Lord's three-year earthly ministry. Matthew, Mark, Luke, and John report Jesus' interactions with people who were disabled with leprosy, blindness, mental illness, speech problems, deafness, and physical impairments. Jesus' Great Commission included them as well, and the church should reflect his concern. In our congregation, is the Great Commission accessible to everyone—even someone with a diagnosis?

1. Regardless of ability, everyone has a soul.

- A person with a disability is first and foremost a person.
- The most valuable part of a person is the soul, and the soul needs to be redeemed and nurtured.
- The Great Commission is clear: Everybody everywhere is invited to hear and respond to the gospel.

2. Regardless of ability, the soul needs salvation.

- The disabilities that cause the most concern in teaching the plan of salvation are mental retardation and similar cognitive delays.
- Persons who are blind can learn Braille, persons who are deaf can "hear" through signs, and people with other disabilities can learn the gospel *if* it's presented in a way that will overcome their negative learning characteristics.
- Are persons with disabilities, especially those with mental retardation, accountable for their sins? Yes, if their mental

age permits it. Can people with mental retardation understand how to become Christians? Yes, if they're taught.

- They have other spiritual needs as well: fellowship, account-
ability, learning God's Word, worship, prayer, giving, and
service.

3. Regardless of ability, persons with cognitive deficiencies *can* be taught the gospel.

- People can establish relationships, lessons can be geared to
the proper level, and appropriate language can be used.
With a lot of prayer and perhaps over a long period of
time, the gospel can be lived and taught.
- Why would we consider those conditions too high a price to
pay to cooperate with the Great Commission?

4. Regardless of ability, everyone has the need to use special gifts for the Lord.

- God has a purpose for all of his children.
- The "weaker member" factor is important
(I Corinthians 12:22).
- Everyone's unique gift helps the kingdom function.

5. Regardless of ability, everyone should be given the opportunity to be a part of the body of Christ, fellowship with God's people, and have the hope of heaven.

- Meeting together with people who share our faith is a part
of being a member of God's family. Sharing meals, time,
joys, troubles, lessons from the Bible, and our love for our
Lord improves our abilities no matter how disabled we are.
- Knowing that someday we will be at peace with our Lord in
heaven adds hope to every day of our lives.

Conclusion

The Great Commission is all-inclusive. The church and her programs
should be accessible to everyone. People with disabilities must be welcome and as actively sought as everyone else to make that inclusion real.

Faith, Friendship, and Disability

Scripture Reading: Luke 5:17-26

Introduction

Friendship is a beautiful word in the Christian community. Having friends that share our faith is a source of encouragement. Furthermore, most of us are part of a church because a friend invited us.

In the world of disability, the friendship connection isn't always present. The story of the four friends who brought their friend to Jesus for healing speaks to the church today (Mark 2:3). Our friendship with people with disabilities can make an eternal difference in their lives. Let's look at four ways of providing friendships that emerge from the story.

1. People with disabilities are valuable.

- It would be interesting to know how the five *became* friends. Did they grow up together? Was the disability a birth defect or the result of an accident? Whatever the cause of the disability, the four saw their friend as valuable and important.
- People with disabilities want affection, acceptance, and accomplishment. Our positive attitude toward them can help.
- Seeing people with disabilities as valuable and worthy of our respect and time will help the friendship connection.

2. Get involved in their lives.

- Nothing happened until one of the four friends got a stretcher and said, "Let's do something."
- The focus of our involvement is their spiritual development. A growing number of churches are opening their hearts and programs to people with disabilities and their families. Children with autism are given buddies to help them adjust in a Sunday school class. Family members can leave their children with special needs at the church building with qualified caregivers while the families go for dinner.
- Disability ministry in a local congregation is a positive way to get involved.

3. Receive from the person with the disability.

- If we complimented these four men for their act of kindness, they might tell us how much their friend did for *them*.
- Real ministry is reciprocal. As we minister to them, the people minister to us.
- In special needs ministry, it is ministry *with* not ministry *to*.
- When our friends with disabilities embrace faith in Jesus, they become our brothers and sisters. They have God-given gifts that can enrich our lives.

4. Provide hope by sharing Jesus.

- The four friends knew the source of true rehabilitation—having the soul touched by Jesus' love.
- Getting our friends with disabilities to Jesus should be our focus. After they know Christ, they should participate in the life of the church.
- Isaiah's prediction will be realized: "Then will the eyes of the blind be opened and the ears of the deaf unstopped. Then will the lame leap like a deer, and the mute tongue shout for joy" (35:5-6).

Conclusion

Find a person in your neighborhood or a family who is dealing with disability. Invite them in friendship to join you at church. Your actions will say, "You are valuable." Get involved with them. Accept their gifts. Tell them about Jesus. Your friendship will make an eternal difference.

14. Special Needs Heroes

Reproducible Bulletin Inserts

by Larry Shallenberger

These ten bulletin inserts about special needs heroes are for you. You may copy as many as you like, as often as you like, and use them any way you like.

They're designed to be two-sided bulletin inserts or fliers and distributed as people enter church. Our hope is that over the course of ten weeks the members of your church who read these personal accounts will recognize that people with special needs have made—and are making—a significant contribution to the church. They're certainly not people you'd want to turn away at the door.

Though—sadly—that's what happens sometimes. It may be because of our attitude toward people with special needs or simply because someone in a wheelchair can't reach or open the door.

Along the way your church members will be challenged to consider how they'd feel if they were to become disabled or if they were disabled and attending your church. This is a low-key, low-pressure way to raise the awareness of readers to the need for special needs ministries in your congregation.

Special Needs Hero

Billy Graham

Billy Graham may always remain the world's favorite evangelist. Dr. Graham has appeared on the Gallup organization's list of "most admired men" forty-five times. Forty-five. That's a lot of admiration!

Billy Graham may also long be remembered as one of the world's most famous sufferers of Parkinson's disease. Parkinson's disease is a debilitating ailment that impairs its sufferers in several ways.

People with Parkinson's disease experience chronic stiffness in their muscles. Some patients complain of chronic arm pain and others experience tremors in their arms, jaws, necks, or faces. Some Parkinson's victims report a loss of balance and dizziness and have difficulty walking.

Billy Graham soldiered through many of these symptoms as well as other health problems brought on by advancing age, continuing to travel and speak in front of huge crowds that often filled entire stadiums. His calling to preach the gospel, expressed through the newly formed Youth for Christ International in the 1940s, continued for more than fifty years.

Graham was one of the first evangelists able to penetrate the Iron Curtain, openly preaching the gospel in public settings. He's preached in person to more than eighty million people and received both the Presidential Medal of Freedom and the Congressional Gold Medal.

Graham has proclaimed the gospel through twenty-three books, Decision magazine (1.4 million circulation), and his *Hour of Decision* radio show. He has further strengthened the church by founding Christianity Today magazine.

Though Graham felt the toll of Parkinson's disease, he continued to hold crusades and attract hundreds of thousands of listeners.

William Martin, author of *Prophet with Honor: The Billy Graham Story*, quotes Graham as saying, "My mind tells me I ought to get out there and go, but I just can't do it. But I'll preach until there is no breath left in my body. I was called by God, and until God tells me to retire, I cannot. Whatever strength I have, whatever time God lets me have, is going to be dedicated to doing the work of an evangelist, as long as I live."

For Further Exploration

- Visit one of the shut-ins of your church—listen and enjoy a conversation about the history of your church. How could your church benefit from hearing these stories of how God has moved in your congregation? How can you help share these stories in ways you will be heard?
- What types of frustrations do you think Billy Graham has experienced as he attempted to continue his ministry in spite of Parkinson's disease?
- How can your church help elderly people with special needs to enjoy their experience at your church?

A Passage to Ponder

"Not that I have already obtained all this, or have already been made perfect, but I press on to take hold of that for which Christ Jesus took hold of me. Brothers, I do not consider myself yet to have taken hold of it. But one thing I do: Forgetting what is behind and straining toward what is ahead, I press on toward the goal to win the prize for which God has called me heavenward in Christ Jesus."

—Philippians 3:12-14

Prayer

Dear God,

Sometimes our bodies and our energy betray us. We fall short of what we want to do for you. We pray for health so we can serve you and tell all those we come in contact with about the joy of knowing you. At times, we're tempted to quit. Help us press on for the prize that is you.

In Jesus' name, amen.

special needs—special ministry
for children's ministry

Special Needs Hero

Don Bartlette

Dr. Don Bartlette has experienced enough abuse, neglect, and physical ailments for bitterness to take hold in his life.

Instead, he's made a career of speaking a message of love and tolerance. Bartlette has presented his workshop "Macaroni at Midnight" over seven thousand times at foster care training sessions, churches, and public schools. Dr. Bartlette has been featured on the Focus on the Family radio program, and Messenger Films is producing a movie based on his life.

Bartlette was born with a severe cleft palate into a poor Chippewa family who lived in the hills of North Dakota. Ashamed of his son's disfigured face, Bartlette's father never called the boy "son." A rugged, athletic man who drank excessively, Bartlette's father beat him violently.

Bartlette was nine before he started attending school. He arrived speaking in grunts and sign language and was daily ridiculed by other children. His peers hit him and spit on him. One teacher forced Bartlette to stay in the janitor's closet rather than the classroom as a way of avoiding disruptions that came with having Bartlette in class. Bartlette moved through the school system in spite of his academic shortcomings because teachers didn't want him in their classrooms for another year.

At twelve, Bartlette was still unable to speak. He became a loner, clothing and feeding himself from the town dump. He committed minor crimes, was arrested, and then sent home on bail—where his father beat him mercilessly.

Bartlette's life turned around when a new woman moved into town. The first day they met, she taught him how to wash a car. Later Bartlette trusted her enough to let her teach him how to use silverware. She then patiently taught him to read, write, and talk.

Asking his benefactor why she was helping him when no one else would, the woman showed Bartlette a Bible.

She arranged for Bartlette to receive plastic surgery. After seven years of tutoring, he graduated as valedictorian of his high school class. He continued with higher education and became a social worker, counselor, and educator.

For Further Exploration

- What personal risks did the woman in Don Bartlette's story assume when she befriended him?
- Imagine that a boy with a cleft palate like Bartlette lived next door to your church. What are some of the risks involved in attempting to reach out to this child? What would some of the benefits be?
- Think through your circle of influence. Who are the people in your life to whom it would be a risk to extend compassion? Commit to praying for these people this week. Ask God if he'd like you to share his love with one of the people on your list.
- Consider watching the film *Patch Adams* (rated PG-13) with a group of people from your church. After the movie, discuss how the risk of getting involved with people affected the life of the main character. Discuss the reason why individuals and churches sometimes pull back from the adventure of touching lives.

A Passage to Ponder

"But a Samaritan, as he traveled, came where the man was; and when he saw him, he took pity on him. He went to him and bandaged his wounds, pouring on oil and wine. Then he put the man on his own donkey, took him to an inn and took care of him."

—Luke 10:33-34

Prayer

Dear God,

Like the travelers in the parable, we're on a journey. As we go, give us courage to see and meet the needs of other travelers on the way. We apologize for times when we have passed people by. Forgive us for ignoring the needs of people for whom you have died. Teach us to be neighbors to the hurting.

In Jesus' name, amen.

Special Needs Hero

Dave Dravecky

Dave Dravecky's career has evolved from player (baseball) to survivor (cancer) to player (baseball) to survivor (cancer) to counselor (life).

Dravecky began his major league baseball career as a starting pitcher for the San Diego Padres. During his fifth year with the Padres, he helped his team reach the World Series. In 1987 Dravecky went to the San Francisco Giants in a blockbuster seven-player swap. Undeterred by being cast off by his former team, Dravecky threw a no-hitter the opening day of the 1988 season.

In October of the same season, doctors detected cancer in Dravecky's pitching arm. Surgeons removed half the muscle in his pitching shoulder, but Dravecky refused to accept that his baseball days were behind him. He began an intense program of rehabilitation, and a year later Dravecky pitched a 4-3 victory over Cincinnati, earning the cheering admiration of both fans and peers. He wrote about his journey in the stirring book *Comeback.*

The cheering evaporated when Dravecky's humerus bone snapped while delivering a pitch in a game against the Montreal Expos. Extensive radiation treatments had weakened the bone, and his dramatic comeback was officially over. Cancer made an unwelcome comeback the following year. The doctors had no choice but to amputate his arm. There would be no second comeback: not for a pitcher with his pitching arm gone.

Today Dravecky is a popular speaker and author. He contributed to the *Encouragement Bible* and has established the national cancer ministry Outreach of Hope. Through his magazine, The Encourager, and Web site, Dravecky provides practical, biblical counsel for cancer and amputation survivors. Several Christian ministries such as Focus on the Family and Promise Keepers have featured Dravecky's story.

Dravecky's baseball comeback may have lasted only for a season. However, his emotional and spiritual comebacks from cancer have forged him into a source of hope for thousands of people who are literally battling for their lives.

For Further Exploration

- Think of a time in your life that was particularly difficult over an extended period. Whom did you turn to for support? How would the situation have turned out had those supportive people not been around—or had refused to help?

- When a family member has a special need, the entire family experiences stress. Take a mental inventory of the programs that your church offers. How can your church provide support for a family stressed by special needs?

- What are some ways your church can provide emotional and practical supports for people who don't have families to rely on? What new programs might help?

A Passage to Ponder

"But God has combined the members of the body and has given greater honor to the parts that lacked it, so that there should be no division in the body, but that its parts should have equal concern for each other. If one part suffers, every part suffers with it; if one part is honored, every part rejoices with it."

—1 Corinthians 12:24b-26

Prayer

Dear God,

Thank you for connecting us as you've knit us all into one body. Help us stop seeing ourselves only as individuals but as part of the church. The joys that affect one of us affect all of us. The pain of one is everyone's pain. In this bigger sense, we lift "our" pain to you. Heal us. Help us work together to support and encourage the weak.

In Jesus' name, amen.

special needs—special ministry
for children's ministry

Special Needs Hero

Dennis Byrd

On November 28, 1992, Dennis Byrd was a specimen of physical prowess. Byrd was a 6-foot-5-inch, 270-pound defensive end for the New York Jets.

On November 29, 1992, Byrd couldn't unclasp his own chinstrap. During a home game against the Kansas City Chiefs, he spun around the offensive line and collided with another teammate while attempting to sack the quarterback. Within seconds of hitting the hard turf, Byrd knew he was paralyzed.

One moment Byrd was an NFL gladiator; the next he was unable to move. As he lay in a hospital bed, Byrd didn't know if he'd ever be able to hold his wife, Ange, or his daughter, Ashtin, again.

As the ambulance rushed him to the hospital, Byrd summoned his faith in God. In his autobiography, *Rise and Walk,* he writes, "It was at that moment, en route to the hospital, that I turned everything over to the Lord, that I put it all in His hands...I had no idea what lay ahead of me, but I knew that this was going to be a test."

Byrd was a quadriplegic. The football-field collision had shattered the fifth-cervical vertebra in his spine. The doctors couldn't promise Byrd he'd ever walk again.

Although he lay limply in bed, Byrd's mind and spirit were active. On a poster board that he could see, the hospital chaplain wrote the words, "For I reckon that the sufferings of this present time are not worthy to be compared with the glory which shall be revealed to us" (Romans 8:18, King James Version).

Byrd spent months in the hospital undergoing experimental therapies and surgeries. All the while his childhood faith was being refined through his fear, discouragement, and intense frustration along the way. Two months after his accident, Byrd was able to take small steps.

Byrd's miraculous rehabilitation captured the nation's attention. The week before the Super Bowl, Bob Costas interviewed Byrd and his wife before a live national audience. Byrd had the opportunity to share how his faith in Jesus was a source of strength during his long months of rehabilitation. Less than a year later, Byrd walked to the middle of Meadowlands Stadium to the cheers of seventy-five thousand fans.

- Dennis Byrd drew from his history with God to get him through dark months of rehabilitation. Schedule a few quiet hours, and journal your history with God. Write down the milestones that you and God have encountered together. How can remembering these times be a source of strength for you in the future?
- Byrd relied on encouragement from his wife, friends, and the hospital chaplain to find the strength to commit to rehab. Why is encouragement so important in overcoming obstacles?
- How can your church be a place of encouragement to those dealing with special needs?

A Passage to Ponder

"Praise be to the God and Father of our Lord Jesus Christ, the Father of compassion and the God of all comfort, who comforts us in all our troubles, so that we can comfort those in any trouble with the comfort we ourselves have received from God."

—2 Corinthians 1:3-4

Prayer

Dear God,

When we're afflicted with suffering, our first response is usually to grumble. Help us to respond to you in faith, trusting that you will comfort us. It's only after we've felt your comfort that we're able to comfort the afflicted around us. We trust your plans, even when we cannot understand them.

In Jesus' name, amen.

OK TO COPY

Special Needs Hero

Frank Peretti

Frank Peretti is famous for penning best-selling novels concerning spiritual warfare. However, long before he wrote about unseen battles, he had battles of his own.

Peretti was born with a life-threatening condition known as cystic hygroma. Cystic hygroma is a birth defect usually found on the neck. A mass growing on a sufferer's neck threatens to close the airway, and the mass often causes the bone structure of the skull and teeth to develop incorrectly.

When Peretti was born, the doctors misdiagnosed the small lump on his neck. The doctors assumed that the forceps used during a harrowing, middle-of-the-night-blizzard delivery caused the lump. Peretti's nervous parents were told that the lump would dissolve within a few weeks. Two months later, doctors performed emergency surgery to remove a baseball-sized lump from Peretti's throat.

At first, the surgery seemed to be successful. Then young Peretti's tongue began to swell out of his mouth. During his neck surgery, the doctors removed some of Peretti's lymph nodes. Consequently, the remaining lymph nodes were forced to secrete an infection into his tongue. A fluid oozed from Peretti's mouth that turned black when it encountered the air.

The enlarged tongue made speech development a torturous task. Seven tongue surgeries carved his tongue into a stub creating a whole new set of problems for Peretti. His speech was slurred, and by the time he went to kindergarten, his tongue again draped from his mouth. The draping tongue, drooling, and black fluid turned Peretti into a target for teasing. And because the cystic hygroma also delayed Frank's physical development, he was unusually small. Only his mother's loving but firm authority kept him in school.

Peretti's family and church were a haven from the daily abuse he suffered at school. Children in Frank's Sunday school class welcomed him as a friend and prayed for his recovery.

Peretti's books for adults, including *This Present Darkness* and *Piercing the Darkness,* have sold in excess of nine million copies, and children have enjoyed his popular Cooper Kids Adventure Series. He's impacting the world through print, speaking engagements, and video production.

For Further Exploration

- Peretti praises his church family for being a safe place for him as a child. What were the potential challenges Peretti's church faced by welcoming his family into their congregation?
- How is your church a safe place for people with special needs?
- How can the children of your church help make your church a safe haven for children with special needs?

A Passage to Ponder

"A man with leprosy came and knelt before him and said, 'Lord, if you are willing, you can make me clean.' Jesus reached out his hand and touched the man."

—Matthew 8:2-3a

Prayer

Dear God,

We're all disfigured in some way. Some of us wear our disfigurements visibly. Some of us wear our scars on the walls of our souls. Please teach us to be gentle with each other. Remind us that our words can be like stones; forgive us for the times we've thrown unkind words at people who are different from us. Use our kind words to build safe havens for the hurting.

In Jesus' name, amen.

Special Needs Hero

Ginny Owens

Ginny Owens discovered the piano at the young age of two—at about the same time that she completely lost her sight. Her difficulty seeing was so evident at birth that her parents and doctors easily noticed her poor vision. Surgeries were attempted, but none saved her sight.

Owens' parents were determined their daughter would have the same experiences that other children enjoyed growing up. In an online interview at www.TodaysChristianMusic.com, Owens recalls "climbing tall trees, riding bikes, roller skating, digging in the back yard determined to make it to China." And music was a large part of her experience.

In spite of her parent's drive that their daughter be no different from any other child, potential employers certainly viewed her as "different." *Too* different to be hired.

Owens graduated from Belmont University, *cum laude,* with a degree in music education—and a requirement to successfully complete student teaching. But when she applied for teaching jobs, principals refused to hire her. Owens believes her blindness prevented her from being hired.

Owens describes her response as "stubborn." She wasn't about to let go of everything that she'd invested in her education. She wrestled with the issues of being a blind person seeking employment.

Then a publisher took an interest in Owens' music. She signed as a writer, then produced a three-song demo album and signed with Michael W. Smith's Rocketown Records in 1999. The same year, she performed at the prestigious Lilith Fair, a concert honoring female artists, in Nashville, Tennessee. Her first album, *Without Condition,* introduced her to the Christian music scene and won her the 2000 Dove Award for "New Artist of the Year." "Blessed," a song she co-wrote with Cindy Morgan, earned her a 2001 Dove Award for "Inspirational Song of the Year."

Several network television shows such as *Felicity, Charmed, Roswell,* and *Get Real* have featured Owens' music.

While Owens resists being classified by her disability, she acknowledges that she has had to make adjustments in the way she connects with her audience. A typical singer uses facial cues to determine how the audience is responding. Owens listens to the audience, guessing whether they're listening.

For Further Exploration

- Close your eyes. Think through what it would take you to accomplish the simple routine of getting dressed in the morning if you were sightless. What systems would you have to put in place for you to be able to wash your clothes, find them in the morning, and dress yourself?
- What would it take for you to be able to attend and participate in church?
- Think through your worship service and Christian education experience. How do these opportunities appeal to senses other than sight? If you were unable to see, would you be able to participate fully?

A Passage to Ponder

"Open my eyes that I may see wonderful things in your law."
—Psalm 119:18

Prayer

Dear God,

We're all blind in some way. We've been blinded by sin, by pride, by greed. We don't see the world accurately. Sometimes we don't see other people at all. Open our spiritual eyes so we become aware of your presence in our lives. Help us see the needs of people around us. Forgive us for choosing to be blind to them.

In Jesus' name, amen.

special needs—special ministry
for children's ministry

Special Needs Hero

Heather Whitestone McCallum

When Heather Whitestone was only eighteen months old, she contracted the Haemophilus influenza virus. To combat the dangerously high fever, doctors gave her two powerful antibiotics.

It's uncertain if it was the fever or the medicine, but Whitestone's hearing was reduced to 5 percent hearing in one ear—and none in the other ear. Doctors told Whitestone's parents their little girl would never speak, drive, or advance beyond a third-grade learning level.

With the help of her parents, Heather Whitestone shattered the limitations her doctors placed on her. At the age of six, she began taking ballet lessons. Her mother taught her to use her limited hearing and to read lips. Following high school she wanted to join a Christian dance company, but submitted to her mother's desire that she attend college. She attended Jackson State University, which didn't have a dance program, so she continued to dance on her own.

Learning dance routines was particularly difficult since she couldn't hear the music's rhythm. She learned to count the music in her head and memorize her dance routines in thirty-second blocks. Through unflagging perseverance, she mastered a single dance routine in a year's time.

When she decided to enter the Miss America Competition, she prepared herself by attending the pageant the year before she planned to enter. She realized that she would be distracted by the crowd noise, and it would interfere with her ability to hear the beginning of her music. Undaunted, she performed in countless nursing homes and churches to train herself to focus while dancing. Her first competition interviews failed because she couldn't understand what the judges were saying. However, Whitestone tried again and won entrance into the pageant.

In front of forty million television viewers, Whitestone used her hard-earned dancing skills to witness to her faith...and she won the title.

In 2002 Whitestone married. She continues to use her position of influence as a former Miss America to spread the gospel with her books *Believing the Promise, Listening With My Heart,* and *Let God Surprise You.*

For Further Exploration

- When someone who can't hear accomplishes something remarkable—such as becoming Miss America—why does it amaze people? What do you think our culture assumes about people who can't hear? can't see? can't speak?
- Imagine attending your worship services as a deaf person. How much of the experience would you be able to appreciate? What elements would you miss?
- How could your church make participating in worship services easier for those who can't hear?

A Passage to Ponder

"Now for this very reason also, applying all *diligence,* in your faith supply moral excellence, and in your moral excellence, knowledge, and in your knowledge, self-control, and in your *self-control*, perseverance, and in your *perseverance*, godliness..."

—2 Peter 1:5-6 (emphasis added)

Prayer

Dear God,

We thank you for Heather Whitestone McCallum's example of faith and determination. Forgive us for letting lesser obstacles keep us from accomplishing what you want us to do. Help us learn from our brothers and sisters who daily face the challenge of dealing with deafness, blindness, and other special needs.

In Jesus' name, amen.

168
special needs—special ministry
for children's ministry

Special Needs Hero

Joni Eareckson Tada

At fifteen years of age, Joni Eareckson placed her faith in Jesus at a Young Life Camp. Three short years later, her fledgling faith was put to the test when she broke her neck in a diving accident. She became a quadriplegic and lost complete use of her hands. Eareckson committed herself to two long years of rehabilitation in order to learn how to hold a paintbrush with her teeth. Among her many talents, she's now an accomplished artist and illustrator.

Eareckson published her autobiography, *Joni,* in 1976. The book shares how Eareckson's faith enabled her to wrestle with the reality that, short of a miracle, she'd remain a quadriplegic the rest of her life.

World Wide Pictures released the movie *Joni* in 1979 and translated it into fifteen languages. Joni and Friends ministry was founded at the same time and has influenced the lives of thousands of disabled people.

Joni married high school history teacher Ken Tada in 1982. Recently Ken retired from teaching and joined the ministry of Joni and Friends.

According to the Joni and Friends Web site, the Wheels for the World program has collected over fourteen thousand used wheelchairs, arranged for their refurbishing, and shipped them overseas. Medical staff fit these wheelchairs to both children and adults.

The National Religious Broadcasters honored her radio program "Joni and Friends" with the "Radio Program of the Year" award. The foundation has created retreat centers for families affected by disability. A sports camp provides specialized training for wheelchair athletes.

Eareckson Tada is a prolific author. Her thirty books have included devotionals, art collections, and children's books. *Tell Me the Promises* and *Tell Me the Truth* both won awards from the Christian publishing industry. She's a columnist for several magazines in Europe.

Prior to her diving accident, Eareckson Tada never could have imagined the tremendous impact that her life would have on thousands of people. Small wonder one of her favorite Bible verses is 2 Corinthians 12:9b, " 'My grace is sufficient for you, for my power is made perfect in weakness.' Therefore I will boast all the more gladly about my weaknesses, so that Christ's power may rest on me."

For Further Exploration

- Take the National Organization on Disability's audit on barriers at www.nod.org. What did you learn about your church, and how inviting is it to those in wheelchairs?
- Borrow several wheelchairs from a health-care provider, and take a field trip of your church. How did you feel as you attempted to navigate your church by wheelchair?
- Eareckson Tada uses her story as a tool to tell others about Christ's work in her life. What is your story? How can you use that story to let others know about Christ?

A Passage to Ponder

"That is why, for Christ's sake, I delight in weaknesses, in insults, in hardships, in persecutions, in difficulties. For when I am weak, then I am strong."

—2 Corinthians 12:10

Prayer

Dear God,

We're weak people...but we hate to admit it. We like to imagine that we have power and influence. But without your power, we're lost, Lord. We invite you to work through our weakness so your power can work through us. We commit to you this power to care for the weak and to uphold the downcast among us.

In Jesus' name, amen.

Special Needs Hero

Phil Keaggy

For Phil Keaggy, less is more. As a guitarist, he does more with nine fingers than most guitarists can accomplish with ten.

Musician magazine ranked Keaggy in their list of the "100 Greatest Guitar Players of the Twentieth Century." His 1990 release *Find Me in These Fields* garnered both a Grammy nomination and the Gospel Music Association's "Instrumental Album of the Year." His albums *Acoustic Sketches, 220, Premium Jams, The Wind and the Wheat, Beyond Nature, Invention, Majesty & Wonder,* and *The Lights of Madrid* have all scored numerous nominations and Dove Awards, the Christian music industry's equivalent of a Grammy.

With nine fingers—not ten.

Keaggy's discography has stretched through thirty years. He's produced some forty instrumental and vocal albums during his illustrious career. Classically inspired pieces, jazz, sixteen-bar rock riffs—he's a top talent no matter what direction the music takes him. And through projects such as "True Believer," he sings the truths of the gospel with the unmistakable clarity of a tent-preacher.

With nine-fingers—not ten.

And that's one of the most amazing things about Keaggy's career: how seldom anyone mentions that he's missing 10 percent of a guitarist's most essential tools.

Like thousands of other children, as a youngster Keaggy expressed an interest in music. His father bought him a nineteen-dollar guitar. And there's no evidence that his parents tried to steer him away from playing guitar in order to protect him from failure or disappointment.

Instead Keaggy's parents allowed their son to pursue his passion with excellence. For Keaggy, excellence was an expression of his spirituality. In an interview in Fingerplay Guitar Magazine, Keaggy says, "I also want to encourage other guitar players to pursue a life of excellence, a life that has spiritual significance."

For Further Exploration

- Phil Keaggy's family was willing to nurture his interest in the guitar, although he had a physical disability. What are some ways that your church can nurture everyone's God-shaped dream—including the dreams of the physically disabled?

- Why do you think most people tend to focus on obstacles instead of opportunities?

- Schedule a time to tour through your church facilities with a group of friends and leaders. Consider inviting a person who uses a wheelchair to join your group. Do your facilities present any obstacles for physically disabled people in your church? What steps can your church take to make your building more welcoming to people with physical disabilities?

A Passage to Ponder

"Love never fails. But where there are prophecies, they will cease; where there are tongues, they will be stilled; where there is knowledge, it will pass away."

—1 Corinthians 13:8

Prayer

Dear God,

You say all things are possible. Please forgive us for focusing on the obstacles instead of the possibilities. Forgive us for viewing people with special needs in terms of problems that need solving. Lord, we know that you have filled every one of us with immense potential and possibilities. We submit ourselves to you and to your power to work inside of us.

We love you and pray in Jesus' name, amen.

special needs—special ministry
for children's ministry

Special Needs Hero

Rick Warren

Adrenaline. Talk with any preaching pastor in America, and you'll hear that the body's natural ability to create adrenaline is a vital part of preaching. Without adrenaline's energizing effects to sustain a pastor's energy level, most sermons would fall flat. In fact, psychologist Archibald Hart suggests that many pastors are *addicted* to the euphoric feeling that adrenaline brings.

Not so for Pastor Rick Warren. When adrenaline rushes through his veins, he feels ill. He was born with a brain disorder that prevents his body from assimilating the chemical. When a stressor triggers the release of the chemical in Warren's body, he feels symptoms such as fainting, headaches, dizziness, temporary blindness, and confusion. These conditions would make it hard for any pastor to fulfill pulpit duties, but Warren is in an especially challenging situation: At Saddleback Community Church in Southern California, he preaches to crowds totaling over thirty-two thousand people every weekend.

In an interview on his Web site, www.pastors.com, Rick Warren writes about why it's painful for him to preach: "The very thing I need to speak to five thousand people at one time is the very thing that harms my body...I think it's part of God's design that the guy who [God] chose to speak at Saddleback is also a guy who is really quite weak."

Treatment is an ongoing issue for Warren. When he was growing up, doctors treated him with epilepsy medication because they didn't know what else to do. The Mayo Clinic is currently involved with Warren's ongoing treatment.

During its first fifteen years, Saddleback Community Church grew from 250 people to 10,000 people—and all without a permanent building. Warren and his teams scrambled to find seventy-nine different locations to host their church. Talk about adrenaline!

Warren continues to preach, speak, and write—he's author of several bestsellers—all while enduring his allergy to adrenaline.

For Further Exploration

- Download a sample stress test at www.stressdiagnosis.com and take the self-inventory. What would your life be like if you suffered an allergy to adrenaline?
- People are more aware of food allergies lately—such as allergies to gluten and peanuts. Ask your kitchen and children's ministries what safety policies are in place to ensure the food your church serves is safe for everyone. If you use wheat-based bread for Communion, what happens to someone who's allergic to gluten in the wheat?
- Unseen disorders, like Rick Warren's allergy, could be mistaken for a character flaw such as a lack of motivation. How should the church go about calling people to excellence without being insensitive to people who may have unseen impairments?

A Passage to Ponder

"But God chose the foolish things of the world to shame the wise; God chose the weak things of the world to shame the strong...so that no one may boast before him."

—1 Corinthians 1:27, 29

Prayer

Dear God,

In our pride we refuse to believe that we are weak. We like to forget that we still struggle with sin. We like to pretend that we can get through life on our own power. We are foolish. Help us to be "poor in spirit." Thank you for loving us, even through the weakness of our pride.

In Jesus' name, amen.

special needs—special ministry
for children's ministry

Epilogue

I Wish I Had Done More
by Kenneth Lay

It was my privilege to know intimately four special needs children during my ministry as a pastor, and their influence continues to impact my spiritual journey.

I learned early that such children have a mission, and as their stories unfold they continually touch lives in a unique way. As I reflect on their mission, I also look back on my own ministry to them and their families. This is my conclusion: I wish I had done more.

Mark was born with serious birth defects, and periodically he had to be hospitalized over one hundred miles away. His father was a public schoolteacher, and in an effort to be of help, I substituted for him on some of those occasions. At other times, I took Mark and his mother to the hospital. I wish I had done more. I wish I had ministered to the depth of the pain and the challenge to the faith of Mark's mother and father.

Jay was born with Down syndrome. When he was very young, I would hold him in my arms as we told the congregation goodbye after the morning worship service. He enjoyed that and so did I. But I wish I had done more. I wish I had put my arms around his daddy. I wish I had hugged his mom. I wish I had been more sensitive to the needs of his sister and brother.

Paul was born with a multitude of problems, including Down syndrome. He lived in another town, and we only saw him on special occasions such as at his brother's wedding when Paul, as the ring bearer, rode his Little Tikes bike down the aisle. I wish I had been more involved in his life through intercessory prayer, letters of encouragement, and more frequent phone calls.

Abby was born with cystic fibrosis and lived for thirteen years. When she died, I held her mother in my arms and cried with her. Her mother was my daughter. I wish I had done the same for the mothers and fathers of all the others. I wish I had shed the tears I felt instead of holding them back in order "to be strong for the family." After all, Jesus wept with his friends at the grave of Lazarus. I have learned that hugs and tears sometimes carry more healing and strength than words of advice.

Special needs children can play a far greater role in our lives and the lives of our churches if we allow them to. Every church and every pastor should be personally involved in disability ministries. It allows the love of God to flow in all directions and produces a bond of heavenly fellowship. It calls for more than empathy; it calls for a sharing of emotions. Children (and their families) with special needs sometimes are ignored and not always loved. The blessing is ours when we love them, accept them, cry with them, and allow them to fulfill their mission.

I wish I had done more.

Kenneth Lay, a retired minister, now teaches Sunday school at First Baptist Church in Edmond, Oklahoma.

special needs—special ministry
for children's ministry